INTRODUCING
ISSUES WITH
OPPOSING
VIEWPOINTS®

The Death Penalty

Lauri S. Friedman, *Book Editor*

GREENHAVEN PRESS
A part of Gale, Cengage Learning

GALE
CENGAGE Learning™

Detroit • New York • San Francisco • New Haven, Conn • Waterville, Maine • London

GALE
CENGAGE Learning

Christine Nasso, *Publisher*
Elizabeth Des Chenes, *Managing Editor*

© 2011 Greenhaven Press, a part of Gale, Cengage Learning

Gale and Greenhaven Press are registered trademarks used herein under license.

For more information, contact:
Greenhaven Press
27500 Drake Rd.
Farmington Hills, MI 48331-3535
Or you can visit our Internet site at gale.cengage.com

For product information and technology assistance, contact us at

Gale Customer Support, 1-800-877-4253
For permission to use material from this text or product, submit all requests online at www.cengage.com/permissions

Further permissions questions can be e-mailed to permissionrequest@cengage.com

Articles in Greenhaven Press anthologies are often edited for length to meet page requirements. In addition, original titles of these works are changed to clearly present the main thesis and to explicitly indicate the author's opinion. Every effort is made to ensure that Greenhaven Press accurately reflects the original intent of the authors. Every effort has been made to trace the owners of copyrighted material.

Cover image by David J. Sams/Stone/Getty Images.

LIBRARY OF CONGRESS CATALOGING-IN-PUBLICATION DATA

The death penalty / Lauri S. Friedman, book editor.
   p. cm. -- (Introducing issues with opposing viewpoints)
 Includes bibliographical references and index.
 ISBN 978-0-7377-4938-0 (hbk.)
 1. Capital punishment--United States--Juvenile literature. 2. Capital punishment--Juvenile literature. I. Friedman, Lauri S.
  HV8699.U5D356 2010
  364.660973--dc22
                                                    2010030748

Printed in the United States of America
1 2 3 4 5 6 7 14 13 12 11 10

Contents

Chapter 3: Is the Death Penalty Applied Fairly?

Foreword

I ndulging in a wide spectrum of ideas, beliefs, and perspectives is a critical cornerstone of democracy. After all, it is often debates over differences of opinion, such as whether to legalize abortion, how to treat prisoners, or when to enact the death penalty, that shape our society and drive it forward. Such diversity of thought is frequently regarded as the hallmark of a healthy and civilized culture. As the Reverend Clifford Schutjer of the First Congregational Church in Mansfield, Ohio, declared in a 2001 sermon, "Surrounding oneself with only like-minded people, restricting what we listen to or read only to what we find agreeable is irresponsible. Refusing to entertain doubts once we make up our minds is a subtle but deadly form of arrogance." With this advice in mind, Introducing Issues with Opposing Viewpoints books aim to open readers' minds to the critically divergent views that comprise our world's most important debates.

Introducing Issues with Opposing Viewpoints simplifies for students the enormous and often overwhelming mass of material now available via print and electronic media. Collected in every volume is an array of opinions that captures the essence of a particular controversy or topic. Introducing Issues with Opposing Viewpoints books embody the spirit of nineteenth-century journalist Charles A. Dana's axiom: "Fight for your opinions, but do not believe that they contain the whole truth, or the only truth." Absorbing such contrasting opinions teaches students to analyze the strength of an argument and compare it to its opposition. From this process readers can inform and strengthen their own opinions, or be exposed to new information that will change their minds. Introducing Issues with Opposing Viewpoints is a mosaic of different voices. The authors are statesmen, pundits, academics, journalists, corporations, and ordinary people who have felt compelled to share their experiences and ideas in a public forum. Their words have been collected from newspapers, journals, books, speeches, interviews, and the Internet, the fastest growing body of opinionated material in the world.

Introducing Issues with Opposing Viewpoints shares many of the well-known features of its critically acclaimed parent series, Opposing Viewpoints. The articles are presented in a pro/con format, allowing readers to absorb divergent perspectives side by side. Active reading questions preface each viewpoint, requiring the student to approach the material thoughtfully and carefully. Useful charts, graphs, and cartoons supplement each article. A thorough introduction provides readers with crucial background on an issue. An annotated bibliography points the reader toward articles, books, and Web sites that contain additional information on the topic. An appendix of organizations to contact contains a wide variety of charities, nonprofit organizations, political groups, and private enterprises that each hold a position on the issue at hand. Finally, a comprehensive index allows readers to locate content quickly and efficiently.

Introducing Issues with Opposing Viewpoints is also significantly different from Opposing Viewpoints. As the series title implies, its presentation will help introduce students to the concept of opposing viewpoints, and learn to use this material to aid in critical writing and debate. The series' four-color, accessible format makes the books attractive and inviting to readers of all levels. In addition, each viewpoint has been carefully edited to maximize a reader's understanding of the content. Short but thorough viewpoints capture the essence of an argument. A substantial, thought-provoking essay question placed at the end of each viewpoint asks the student to further investigate the issues raised in the viewpoint, compare and contrast two authors' arguments, or consider how one might go about forming an opinion on the topic at hand. Each viewpoint contains sidebars that include at-a-glance information and handy statistics. A Facts About section located in the back of the book further supplies students with relevant facts and figures.

Following in the tradition of the Opposing Viewpoints series, Greenhaven Press continues to provide readers with invaluable exposure to the controversial issues that shape our world. As John Stuart Mill once wrote: "The only way in which a human being can make some approach to knowing the whole of a subject is by hearing what can be said about it by persons of every variety of opinion and studying all modes in which it can be looked at by every character of mind. No wise man ever acquired his wisdom in any mode but this." It is to this principle that Introducing Issues with Opposing Viewpoints books are dedicated.

Introduction

Since the death penalty was reinstated in 1976, opponents have argued for its abolition using many tactics. They frequently assert that the death penalty constitutes cruel and unusual punishment, that it fails to deter crime, that it risks executing the innocent, and that it is an immoral and unjust response to crime. But the 2008 recession offered opponents a new way to convince their fellow citizens that the death penalty should be abandoned: its high price. Indeed, as states slashed budgets and struggled to meet rising costs, the death penalty was cast primarily as an issue not of morality or criminal deterrence, but of cost.

A 2009 study undertaken by the Death Penalty Information Center (DPIC) exposed the high price of the death penalty in the context of the nationwide recession. Its thorough and widely reported analysis of U.S. Bureau of Justice Statistics data, taken from thirty-three urban counties nationwide, revealed that death penalty costs can average $10 million more per year per state than life sentences.

One reason the death penalty is so expensive is that carrying out a criminal execution is a notoriously slow process—on average, inmates spend about ten years on death row, but some have spent as long as twenty years waiting to be executed. This is because after a criminal is sentenced to death, numerous appeals are allowed in which lawyers attempt to postpone the inmate's death sentence, or have it repealed entirely. Appeals are part of an effort to ensure the right person is being put to death—given the irreversibility of the death penalty, every effort is made to ensure that no mistakes were made during the trial, but this is a time-consuming and expensive endeavor. A drawn-out appeals process also allows inmates the chance to repent for their crimes. Indeed, sometimes stays of execution are granted because after fifteen or so years in prison, an inmate is believed to show acceptable remorse for the crime. He also might have bettered himself by dedicating himself to God or excelling in prison education programs. These activities are sometimes enough to convince a judge to overturn the death sentence and let the inmate live out his days in prison. No matter the reason, however, the drawn-out appeals process makes the death penalty the most expensive punishment available.

In some states, the price tag of an execution is shockingly high. In California, for example, it costs about $137 million per year to maintain the death penalty system. Yet although hundreds of people sit on the state's death row, executions very rarely take place—just eleven people have been executed there since the death penalty was reinstated in the late 1970s. According to the DPIC, the high cost of the rarely used death penalty system makes the average price tag of each execution a whopping $250 million. Put another way, the state could save an estimated $126 million per year if it abolished the death penalty and replaced capital sentences with life in prison without parole.

Considering California's budget woes have caused it to slash healthcare, education, and other budgets, some people view the state's death penalty system as a financial albatross that gives little back to a struggling state. "The outrageous price that taxpayers bear in order to kill a handful of prisoners has been thrown into sharp relief," said Lance Lindsay, executive director of the abolitionist group Death Penalty Focus. "It is utterly irresponsible to invest hundreds of millions of dollars to expand death rows when our schools, our health care, our environment, and everything we value in our communities face a slow painful demise."[1]

The cost of the death penalty was found to be significant in other struggling states, too. For example, Maryland spends about $37 million per execution, while Florida spends an average of $24 million per execution. As law professor Corinna Barrett Lain puts it, "Vengeance comes at a high price"[2]—a price that many states may no longer be able to afford to pay. Interestingly, Lain points out that in the past, politicians who supported the death penalty were hailed for being tough on crime; in the context of the recession, however, politicians who support the death penalty are being cast by death penalty opponents as fiscally irresponsible and wasteful.

The costs of the death penalty are all the more staggering when one realizes that a large percentage of death penalty cases never actually end up resulting in execution. In some cases sentences are commuted; in others, defendants die in prison, either of natural causes or from suicide. Therefore, a life sentence is often the end result of many death penalty convictions anyway, but for three or four times the price. "This is an extremely wasteful process," write the authors of the 2009 DPIC report. "In most cases a life sentence could have been obtained at the outset of the case for a fraction of the cost."[3] In fact, the DPIC reports that 68 percent of death penalty cases are reversed at some point in the appeals process—when retried, 82 percent of these cases result in a life sentence or less.

To what extent the recession has caused states to rethink their commitment to the death penalty is just one of the issues explored in *Introducing Issues with Opposing Viewpoints: The Death Penalty.* Other classic issues—such as whether the death penalty deters crime, is a fair punishment, is racially biased, or constitutes a violation of human rights—are explored in articles by passionate, expert voices on the topic. Guided reading questions and essay prompts lead readers to form their own opinions on this timeless critical issue.

Notes

1. Lance Lindsay, "We Can't Afford the Death Penalty," New America Media.com, March 4, 2009. http://news.ncmonline.com/news/ view_article.html?article_id=0b51d00d8e7f9c65f192139df5ffd315.
2. Corinna Barrett Lain, "The New Case Against the Death Penalty," *Christian Science Monitor*, May 11, 2009. www.csmonitor.com/ 2009/0511/p09s01-coop.html.
3. Death Penalty Information Center, *Smart on Crime: Reconsidering the Death Penalty in a Time of Economic Crisis*, October 2009, p. 12. www.deathpenaltyinfo.org/documents/CostsRptFinal.pdf.

Chapter 1

Should the Death Penalty Be Legal?

The death penalty has been and remains one of society's most controversial issues.

Viewpoint

1

The Death Penalty Should Be Legal

Jeff Jacoby

In the following viewpoint Jeff Jacoby explains why he believes the death penalty should be legal. In his opinion, the death penalty is the only appropriate punishment for murder. When a murderer strikes, he or she robs his or her victim—and the victim's loved ones—of life, love, liberty, and happiness. Jacoby also cites studies that show that having the death penalty as punishment reduces the number of murders that are committed. So not only does Jacoby think the death penalty honors the lives of those who have died, it also prevents other people from losing their lives. He concludes that too much effort is spent trying to keep guilty criminals alive, and not enough attention is paid to the lives lost at their cruel hands.

Jacoby is a columnist for the *Boston Globe.*

"When the death penalty is unavailable, more innocent victims die."

Jeff Jacoby, "Life and Death in New Jersey," *Boston Globe*, December 19, 2007. Reprinted with permission.

AS YOU READ, CONSIDER THE FOLLOWING QUESTIONS:
  1. Who is Kristin Huggins, and how does she factor into the author's argument?
  2. How many murders does each execution prevent, according to Jacoby?
  3. What percentage of New Jersey residents does Jacoby say favor retaining the death penalty as a punishment for violent crimes?

When Governor Jon Corzine signed legislation repealing New Jersey's death penalty on Monday, there were many people for whom he had good words.

In what *The New York Times* called "an extended and often passionate speech," Corzine praised the members of the Death Penalty Study Commission who had recommended repeal. He saluted the "courageous leadership" of the state legislators who had voted for it, mentioning eight of them by name. He thanked New Jerseyans for Alternatives to the Death Penalty, an activist group, for having "put pressure on those of us in public service to stand up and do the right thing." He proclaimed himself "eternally grateful" to other anti-death-penalty organizations, especially the New Jersey Catholic Conference and the ACLU. He acknowledged "the millions of people across our nation and around the globe who reject the death penalty." He noted politely that there are "good people" who support capital punishment and opposed the bill. He even quoted Martin Luther King Jr.

But there were some people Corzine forgot to mention.

The governor forgot Kristin Huggins. She was the 22-year-old graphic artist kidnapped in 1992 by Ambrose Harris, who stuffed her into the trunk of her car, then let her out in order to rape her and shoot her twice—once in the back of her head, once point-blank in the face.

The governor forgot Irene Schnaps, a 37-year-old widow butchered by Nathaniel Harvey in 1985. After breaking into her apartment and robbing her, he killed her with 15 blows to the head, using a "hammer-like" weapon with such violence that he fractured her skull, broke her jaw, and knocked out her teeth.

The governor forgot Megan Kanka, who was just 7 years old when she was murdered by a neighbor, Jesse Timmendequas. A convicted sex offender, Timmendequas lured Megan into his house by offering to show her a puppy. Then he raped her, smashed her into a dresser, wrapped plastic bags around her head, and strangled her with a belt.

In fact, the governor forgot to mention any of the victims murdered by the men on New Jersey's death row. He signed an order reducing the killers' sentences to life in prison, and assured his audience "that these individuals will never again walk free in our society." But he spoke not a word about any of the men, women, and children who will never again walk at all—or smile, or dream, or breathe—because their lives were brutally taken from them by the murderers the new law spares.

That's the way it so often is with death-penalty opponents like Corzine: In their zeal to keep the guilty alive, they forget the innocents who have died. Their conscience is outraged by the death penalty,

In December 2007 New Jersey governor Jon S. Corzine holds up a bill he has just signed that eliminates the state's death penalty statute.

"Murder victims reply to lethal injection," cartoon by Linda Boileau, www.CartoonStock.com. Copyright © Linda Boileau. Reproduction rights obtainable from www.CartoonStock.com.

but only when it is lawfully applied to convicted murderers after due process of law. The far more frequent "death penalty"—the one imposed unlawfully on so many murder victims, often with wanton cruelty —doesn't disturb their conscience nearly so much.

Nor do their consciences seem overly troubled by the additional lives lost when capital punishment is eliminated.

A widening sheaf of studies (some by scholars who personally oppose the death penalty) have found that each time a murderer is executed, between 3 and 18 additional homicides are deterred. To mention just one example, University of Houston professors Dale Cloninger and Roberto Marchesini studied the effect of the death-penalty moratorium declared by Illinois Governor George Ryan in 2000, and Ryan's subsequent commutation of every death-row inmate's sentence. Result:

an estimated 150 additional murders in Illinois over the subsequent 48 months.

New Jersey hasn't executed anyone since 1963, so the new law may be largely symbolic. But there is nothing symbolic about all the blood shed since the death penalty was abandoned 44 years ago. In 1963, there were 181 homicides in the Garden State. By 1970 there were more than 400, and by 1980, more than 500. In 2002, state officials calculated that on average, a murder was committed in New Jersey every 25 hours and 41 minutes.

While the murder rate since 2000 has declined modestly across the country, it has "jumped 44 percent in Jersey, up from 3.4 murders per 100,000 people to 4.9," writes Steven Malanga of the Manhattan Institute. "Jersey's increase in murders has been the sixth-highest in the country."

FAST FACT

According to the Bureau of Justice Statistics, 65 percent of death row inmates had a prior felony conviction at the time they committed murder; 8.4 percent had a prior homicide conviction.

That may explain why 53 percent of the state's residents opposed the death-penalty repeal, according to a new Quinnipiac poll, while 78 percent favored retaining it for "the most violent cases." Perhaps they grasp the truth that eludes the politicians in Trenton: When the death penalty is unavailable, more innocent victims die.

EVALUATING THE AUTHOR'S ARGUMENTS:

Jeff Jacoby's argument hinges on the idea that it is a waste of energy—and morally wrong—to save the lives of murderers. What do you think? Is it wrong to try to save the life of a murderer? Why or why not?

The Death Penalty Should Be Illegal

Sarah Tofte

"When it comes to the death penalty, nothing about the process, from conviction to killing, has ever been just."

In the following viewpoint Sarah Tofte argues that the death penalty should be outlawed. She bases her argument on the suggestion that people who are executed feel pain during the process. She argues that lethal injection—the most common method of execution, in which a person is given a fatal combination of drugs—is actually a very painful way to die, despite its reputation for offering a painless and peaceful death. Although a prisoner looks as if he is drifting off to sleep, in reality, says Tofte, he is experiencing excruciating pain. Furthermore, says Tofte, many executions go awry, drawing out the prisoner's death in an unnecessarily cruel way. All of these factors cause Tofte to characterize the death penalty as cruel and unusual punishment. Since there is no way to painlessly or peacefully take a human life, she concludes the death penalty should be illegal.

Tofte is a researcher for Human Rights Watch, a global organization that monitors human rights abuses. She is the coauthor of

Sarah Tofte, "Is There a Humane Way to Put Someone to Death?" HuffingtonPost.com, October 31, 2007. Reproduced by permission of the author.

the anti-death-penalty report *So Long as They Die: Lethal Injections in the United States.*

AS YOU READ, CONSIDER THE FOLLOWING QUESTIONS:
1. How does the author say lethal injection came to be used in executions?
2. What is potassium chloride and under what circumstances is it allowed to be used in veterinary medicine, according to Tofte?
3. How many botched executions does the author say have been recorded since 1982?

There was a time when public debate about the death penalty in the United States focused on concerns about racial discrimination, lack of competent counsel for indigent defendants, and executing the innocent. But . . . the death penalty debate has shifted to how we put the condemned to death.

Those who support the death penalty argue that lethal injection is the best way to "administer death." Even if the condemned person experiences a few minutes of excruciating pain, it is humane enough for a convicted murderer. Some of those opposed to the death penalty worry that if lethal injection is replaced by a truly pain-free method, the public's appetite for executions will grow. Both sides agree that a debate about lethal injection will get us nowhere, but in fact, having the debate is useful, because the story of lethal injection mirrors that of the death penalty itself.

The History of Lethal Injection

Botched lethal injections are—like wrongful convictions and incompetent defense attorneys—the product of an astonishing history of negligence, incompetence, and irresponsibility by state officials responsible for implementing a punishment that the public supports, but doesn't want to know too much about.

Lethal injections look peaceful and painless—which is why all but one of the 38 death penalty states have adopted them to replace the more gruesome spectacles of execution by hanging, firing squad, poison gas, or electrocution. But looks can be deceiving. With lethal

Where Is the Death Penalty Legal?

As of 2010, 35 states—plus the federal government and the U.S. military—retained the death penalty.

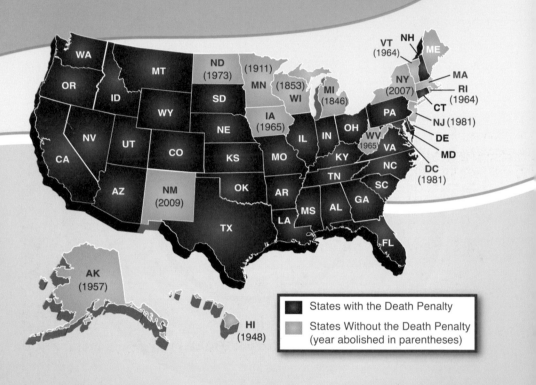

WA

MT

OR

ID

ND (1973)

(1911)

MN (1853)

SD

WI (1846)

MI

VT (1964)

NH

ME

NY (2007)

MA

RI (1964)

CT

NJ (1981)

DE

MD

DC (1981)

WY

NE

IA (1965)

IL

IN

OH

WV 1965

PA

NV

UT

CO

KS

MO

KY

VA

CA

AZ

NM (2009)

OK

AR

TN

NC

SC

MS

AL

GA

TX

LA

FL

AK (1957)

HI (1948)

■ States with the Death Penalty

■ States Without the Death Penalty (year abolished in parentheses)

* In March 2009 New Mexico voted to abolish the death penalty. However, the repeal was not retroactive, leaving two people on the state's death row.

Taken from: Death Penalty Information Center, 2010.

injection, the condemned prisoner is strapped to a gurney and injected with a massive dose of the anesthetic sodium pentothal, which should render him unconscious and stop his breathing. Next he is injected with pancuronium bromide, a drug that paralyzes the muscles, including the lungs and diaphragm. Finally, he is injected with potassium chloride, which should bring swift cardiac arrest.

All of the states that use lethal injection copied this bizarre and dangerous drug protocol from Texas, the national leader in executions, which itself had simply taken the idea from an Oklahoma medical examiner with no pharmacology experience who concocted the protocol in 1977.

Cruel and Unusual Punishment

When the drugs in the three-drug lethal injection protocol are administered properly, the prisoner should be motionless—as well as unable to feel pain—within a minute or two. But execution logs from

The lethal injection room at the Florida State Prison is shown here. Death penalty opponents say that this method of execution is painful and cruel.

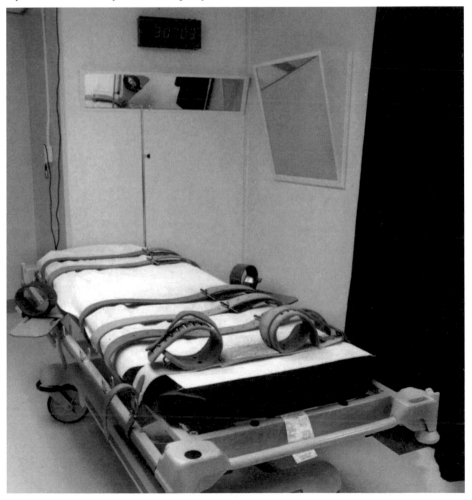

California and North Carolina reveal body movements inconsistent with the proper administration of the lethal injection drugs, particularly the anesthetic. If the prisoners were not sufficiently anesthetized, they may have felt themselves suffocating from the pancuronium bromide, or they may have felt excruciating pain as the potassium chloride coursed its way through their veins to their heart.

Indeed, potassium chloride is so painful that US veterinary guidelines prohibit its use on domestic animals unless a veterinarian first ensures that they are deeply unconscious. But most states do not require anyone to stay at the condemned prisoner's side to make sure he is in fact deeply anesthetized and unconscious before the second and third drugs are administered.

Botched Executions

It should not be surprising that since 1982, states have recorded at least 40 visibly botched executions, in which prisoners showed physical distress during the process—not to mention executions where the prisoner may have felt pain but was unable to express it because of the paralytic drug. Court records in the handful of states where lethal injection is being challenged reveal a sorry litany of incompetence and bungling.

And when things have gone wrong during an execution, states have done little to fix the problem. States react to questions raised about lethal injection the same way they react to claims of other death penalty injustices —with barely disguised indifference. When courts or governors have ordered states to review their execution protocols because of evidence that they may put prisoners at risk of unnecessary pain, state officials chose not to undertake a careful inquiry, but rather made superficial changes that fail to address the inherent flaws of the three-drug protocol. States have been advised of—and routinely rejected—a one-drug protocol, the administration of a massive dose of a long-acting barbiturate. The reason? Although the inmate would not experience any physical pain, it would take him as long as 40 minutes to die, which would be difficult for the execution team and witnesses to watch.

The Death Penalty Will Always Be Inhumane

If the United States is going to retain the death penalty, it must ensure that executions are conducted in as pain-free a manner as possible. But there is no neat, easy, antiseptic way to kill a human being. The lethal injection debate brings this reality into sharp relief, and forces the public to acknowledge that when it comes to the death penalty, nothing about the process, from conviction to killing, has ever been just.

That's why the more we talk about what executions actually look and feel like, the more public support for the death penalty falls away as we grapple with the graphic details of the killing process. No matter how pain-free we make an execution, it will always be taking a human life. And it will always be inhumane.

EVALUATING THE AUTHOR'S ARGUMENTS:

Sarah Tofte uses history, facts, and examples to make her argument that the death penalty should be illegal. She does not, however, use any quotations to support her point. If you were to rewrite this article and insert quotations, what authorities might you quote? Where would you place these quotations to bolster the points Tofte makes?

Viewpoint
3

The Death Penalty Should Be Legal Because It Deters Crime

David Frum

"Restore the death penalty, and you restore safety."

Legalizing the death penalty helps keep crime low, argues David Frum in the following viewpoint. Frum cites statistics that show a connection between a legalized death penalty and lower murder rates. He says that although the death penalty cannot prevent every murder from taking place, its adoption sends a message to criminals that society will not stand for their actions. It tells criminals they will be given the ultimate punishment, and in Frum's opinion, this keeps at least some of them from breaking the law. Frum concludes that letting society threaten criminals with the death penalty keeps cities—and their residents—safe.

Frum is a resident fellow at the American Enterprise Institute, a conservative public policy research institute dedicated to preserving and strengthening government, private enterprise, and vital cultural and political institutions.

AS YOU READ, CONSIDER THE FOLLOWING QUESTIONS:
1 How many fewer murders does the author say took place in 2005 than in 1995?
2. What was the "great havoc" and how does it factor into the author's argument?
3. What does Frum say is now the safest large city in America? In what year did this city reinstate the death penalty?

D o you still get your ideas about American crime from American cop shows? If so, your ideas may be a little out of date. Over the past decade, American cities have become suddenly and dramatically safer.

Between 1995 and 2005, the number of murders in the United States dropped from nearly 25,000 a year to under 15,000. An American was less likely to be murdered in 2005 than in 1960. And the total rate of criminal victimisation tumbled to its lowest level since records began in 1974.

It would be rash to credit the death penalty alone for this triumph. But it would equally be wrong to deny capital punishment its share of the credit.

The Effect of Decriminalising Crime

When crime is punished lightly, criminals feel empowered—and crime proliferates. In the 1960s, for example, US courts placed new restrictions on police, raised new barriers to criminal prosecution, and shortened sentences for the convicted. As crime rates surged between 1960 and 1969, the number of prisoners actually declined.

It was as if the US had decriminalised crime. What happened next has been described by one American writer as "the great havoc": a collapse of order that ravaged once great cities like Detroit and exacted widespread economic and social costs. In 1974, one US household out of three said it was a victim of crime, and crime eclipsed inflation, unemployment, Vietnam and Watergate as the number one concern of American voters.

The Death Penalty Makes a Comeback

In a democracy, the number one concern of voters gets attention. Aggressive politicians, especially Republicans, began to run for office promising action on crime: more police, tougher sentences—and the return of the death penalty. In 1974, the Supreme Court effectively overturned a 1972 decision against the death penalty and soon the worst offenders were being sentenced to die. The first of the "new" death sentences was carried out in 1977 in Utah.

Yet while execution was often sought after 1974, for nearly two decades it was rarely imposed. Procedural delays and manoeuvring by lawyers extended stays on death row from six, to nine, to a peak of 11 years.

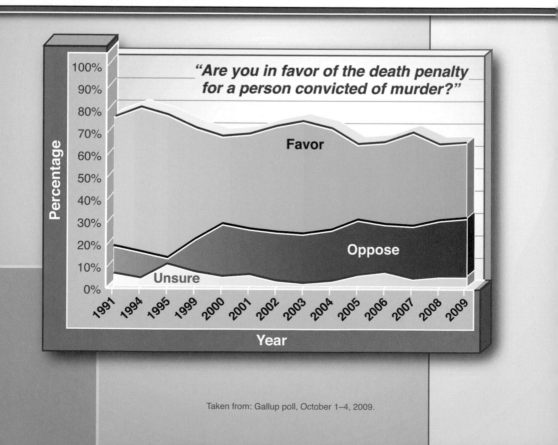

Americans Continuously Support the Death Penalty

Polls taken by Gallup show that year after year, Americans continue to think the death penalty is an appropriate punishment for murder, in part because it deters crime.

"Are you in favor of the death penalty for a person convicted of murder?"

Favor

Oppose

Unsure

Percentage

Year

Taken from: Gallup poll, October 1–4, 2009.

And through it all, public opinion in favour of the death penalty intensified—and with it, the swing to the political right. By 1994, nearly 80% of Americans supported the death penalty. That year the Republicans recaptured both houses of Congress from the Democrats for the first time since 1952. The year before, the Republican Rudolph Giuliani won the mayoralty of New York on a get-tough-on-crime platform. Giuliani supported the death penalty. So did the Republican governor of New York, George Pataki. In 1995, New York would become the 38th state to restore its death penalty. In 1994, the number of executions rose above 20 a year for the first time. Perhaps not coincidentally, 1994 was also the year in which US crime rates—led by those of New York City—began to turn dramatically and decisively down.

> ## FAST FACT
>
> Studies from Emory University, the University of Colorado–Denver, the University of Houston, and others have found that between three and eighteen lives are saved by every execution.

One of Many Law Enforcement Tools

It would be an exaggeration to credit the death penalty alone for the improvement. In the two decades since 1974, more than 400,000 Americans have been murdered—and barely 1000 of their killers have been executed. In no year since the restoration of the death penalty has the number of Americans executed exceeded the number killed by lightning.

So rare a punishment cannot qualify as a deterrent. Nor can it function as a tool of ultimate justice. Many horrendous murderers escape execution.

What the death penalty does do, however, is express as forcefully as society can—both to criminals and law-abiding citizens—that the authorities take crime seriously. It is not a substitute for all the other tools needed to defeat crime: more police and patrols, stricter laws, longer sentences and better economic opportunities.

If societies want to wind back crime, however, they need to begin by sending a clear message that the sheriff is back in town—that crime

David Frum (pictured) argues in this viewpoint that the death penalty is an excellent deterrent that keeps Americans safe.

won't be tolerated and will be punished to the full extent of the law. And nothing broadcasts that message like restoration of the most extreme punishment.

It is striking that Britain has imported many of the best US crime-fighting methods (but not the death penalty), only to see its rates of crime and violence continue to deteriorate. On some level, the bad guys don't yet take the law seriously.

The Death Penalty Ensures Safety

And as a society becomes safer, it can afford to again rediscover some leniency. Support for the death penalty has begun to decline again in the US. The number of executions is beginning to trend down. Yet crime levels remain low and continue to decline further: New York is now very nearly the safest 100,000-plus city in the US and probably one of the safest big cities in the world.

Restore the death penalty, and you restore safety. Restore safety, and everything becomes possible. Refuse the death penalty, and the job of reimposing legal order becomes much more difficult: citizens live in fear, trust in authority and law fade.

There may be another way of protecting society. But why ignore success?

> ## EVALUATING THE AUTHOR'S ARGUMENTS:
>
> David Frum supports his argument that the death penalty deters crime by offering statistics that show a connection between lower murder rates and increased executions. Was his use of these statistics effective? Did it convince you that the death penalty deters crime? Use evidence from the text in your answer.

The Death Penalty Does Not Deter Crime

Warren Richey

"The death penalty does little to prevent violent crimes."

Warren Richey is a staff writer for the *Christian Science Monitor*, a national newspaper. In the following viewpoint Richey presents a poll that shows that the death penalty does not deter crime. He explains that it is very expensive to execute a prisoner and that carrying out the death penalty has cost at least $2 billion since 1976. Richey also explains the findings of a Death Penalty Information Center report that states that perpetrators rarely consider the consequences when engaged in violent crimes, and therefore the death penalty does little to deter violence. The article also reveals that New Mexico has abolished the death penalty and eleven state legislatures have introduced bills calling for an end to capital punishment.

AS YOU READ, CONSIDER THE FOLLOWING QUESTIONS:
1. Who is Richard Dieter, and how does he factor into the author's argument?
2. According to a 2008 study cited by Richey, how much was California spending per year on capital cases?
3. How much money would California save if it instituted a comparable system that sentenced offenders to life without parole instead of the death penalty, according to the author?

A group opposing capital punishment is urging government officials to reassess the costs and benefits of the death penalty in light of America's economic troubles.

State and local governments facing dire budget crunches can realize substantial savings by replacing capital punishment with a regime that sentences the worst offenders to life in prison without parole, according

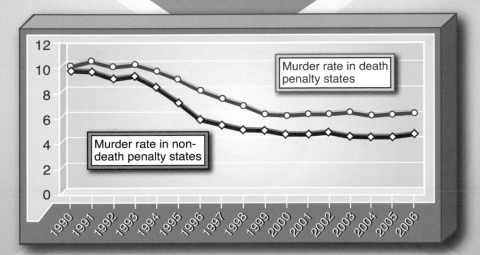

The Death Penalty Is Not a Deterrent

The murder rate in non-death-penalty states has remained consistently lower than the rate in states with the death penalty.

Murder rate in death penalty states

Murder rate in non-death penalty states

Taken from: Amnesty International USA, November 2008, "Crime in the United States," Federal Bureau of Investigation, 2006, and the Death Penalty Information Center.

to a report released [on October 20, 2009,] by the Death Penalty Information Center (DPIC).

The number of death sentences handed down in the United States has dropped from roughly 300 a year in the 1990s to 115 a year more recently. Executions are falling off at the same rate, the report says.

In the meantime, some 3,300 inmates remain on death row.

Death Penalty Expenses

"[T]he death penalty is turning into a very expensive form of life without parole," said Richard Dieter, DPIC executive director, in a statement. "At a time of budget shortfalls, the death penalty cannot be exempt from reevaluation alongside other wasteful government programs that no longer make sense."

Despite the report's findings, the death penalty has the support of most Americans. According to an October 2008 Gallup survey, 64 percent of Americans favor the death penalty for a person convicted of murder. Thirty percent oppose it.

Only once in the past 70 years (in 1966–67) did more Americans oppose capital punishment than support it, the poll results show. In that time span, 47 percent opposed it, while 42 percent supported it.

The DPIC study does not address American attitudes toward capital punishment. Instead, the report focuses on the economic costs.

A 2008 study in California found that the state was spending $137 million a year on capital cases. A comparable system that instead sentenced the same offenders to life without parole would cost $11.5 million, says the DPIC report, citing the study's estimates.

New York spent $170 million over nine years on capital cases before repealing the death penalty. No executions were carried out there.

Anti-death-penalty advocates, such as this woman, point to numerous studies that indicate the death penalty does not deter crime.

New Jersey spent $253 million over 25 years with no executions. That state also repealed capital punishment.

Some officials may be tempted to try to cut capital-punishment costs, notes the DPIC report, but many of those costs reflect Supreme Court-mandated protections at the trial and appeals-court levels. "The choice today is between a very expensive death penalty and one that risks falling below constitutional standards," the report says.

Nationwide, the report estimates, at least $2 billion has been spent since 1976 for costs that wouldn't have been incurred if the severest penalty were life in prison. The figure is based on an estimate in a 1993 North Carolina study that found the average extra cost of a death sentence in this state was $300,000. The average extra cost of capital punishment is significantly higher in several other states like California, Florida, and Maryland, the report says.

Bills calling for an end to capital punishment have been introduced in 11 state legislatures this year [2009]. Also this year, New Mexico abolished the death penalty, and Maryland narrowed its use. The Connecticut governor vetoed a law that would have ended capital punishment.

The DPIC report includes the results of a recent poll of 500 police chiefs nationwide. Fifty-seven percent of the chiefs polled said they agreed with the statement that the death penalty does little to prevent violent crimes because perpetrators rarely consider the consequences when engaged in violence.

Thirty-nine percent of police chiefs disagreed with this statement.

The DPIC study concludes that capital punishment is a wasteful, expensive program that no longer makes sense. "The promised benefits from the death penalty have not materialized," the report says. "If more states choose to end the death penalty, it will hardly be missed, and the economic savings will be significant."

EVALUATING THE AUTHOR'S ARGUMENTS:

In this viewpoint Warren Richey uses statistics from a number of reports, polls, and surveys. Do you think this makes his argument more effective? Why or why not?

Life in Prison Is a Good Alternative to the Death Penalty

Jon Streeter, Bill Hing, and Diane Bellas

"The past 30 years have shown that permanent imprison- ment succeeds where the death penalty fails."

In the following viewpoint Jon Streeter, Bill Hing, and Diane Bellas argue that the death penalty is a broken system that cannot be fixed. They say that too much money is wasted on trying and executing prisoners and that the state can never be sure it is not mistakenly executing an innocent person. In fact, say Streeter, Hing, and Bellas, it is quite possible an innocent person could be executed given the poor legal representation many death row defendants receive. Given these problems, the authors suggest the death penalty be replaced with life in prison with no possibility of parole. In their view, permanent imprisonment accomplishes the same things as the death penalty but without the cost and risk. Permanent imprisonment gets criminals off the streets, offers a severe and unbending punishment, and ensures

Jon Streeter, Bill Hing, and Diane Bellas, "Replace Death Penalty with Permanent Imprisonment," *San Francisco Chronicle*, June 25, 2009. Reproduced by permission of the authors.

that murderers will never be able to strike again. For all these reasons, they recommend abolishing the death penalty and sentencing society's worst criminals to life in prison without parole.

Streeter, Hing, and Bellas served on the California Commission on the Fair Administration of Justice. Streeter was vice chairman of the commission and is a partner at the firm of Keker & Van Nest. Hing is a professor at the University of California–Davis School of Law. Bellas is the public defender of Alameda County in California.

AS YOU READ, CONSIDER THE FOLLOWING QUESTIONS:

1. On average, how long do the authors say it takes a death penalty case to move through the courts?
2. How long do Streeter, Hing, and Bellas say a person sentenced to death in California will wait before being appointed an attorney to appeal his death penalty conviction?
3. How much do the authors say it would cost to build a new facility to house people on California's death row?

A fter spending four years on the California Commission on the Fair Administration of Justice, we were pleased to see state Sen. Tom Harmon, R-Huntington Beach, cite our commission's report on the death penalty in his June 15 [2009] Open Forum piece, "Legal Stalling Packs Death Row." We are concerned, however, that Harmon did not disclose the reasons we concluded that California's death penalty is not working. He also failed to disclose that it will cost more than $230 million a year to fix it.

A "Broken and Unworkable" System

The commission was created by the [California] Senate to investigate the problems of wrongful convictions and wrongful executions. After issuing eight reports on the causes of wrongful convictions, we turned our attention to the administration of the death penalty. Ours was the first comprehensive analysis of the problems with California's death penalty, the reforms needed, the possible alternatives and the costs.

As the senator states, "the death penalty system in California is broken and unworkable." We found that it now takes an average of 25 years for death penalty cases to move through the mandatory court review process. However, the reason these appeals take so long is not because of "legal maneuverings." The primary cause of these delays is the lack of attorneys willing to take these cases and the lack of court staff to review them. A person sentenced to death today in California will wait eight to 10 years before an attorney will be appointed to represent him in a legal challenge to his conviction. Without an attorney, there are no legal maneuverings at all.

Once an attorney is appointed, the case is investigated and briefs are filed in court. Then it will be three to five years before the California Supreme Court has time to review the case. The court has a backlog of 80 cases waiting for its review. Why? The court does not have the time or staff to review the cases more quickly.

We Risk Executing Innocents

But long delays are not the only problem plaguing our death penalty system. Our commission concluded that California remains at risk of executing an innocent person. We recommended a series of reforms to ensure that innocent people are not wrongfully convicted or sentenced to death. The Legislature passed several of these measures, but the governor vetoed them all, three years in a row.

Our commission also found a significant problem with poor quality legal work in death penalty cases. We were shocked to learn that the federal courts reverse two out of three death penalty cases because of the poor performance of the attorneys. In too many cases, poor people are ending up on death row because their lawyers do not have the resources needed to properly investigate and defend the case.

The Death Penalty Costs Too Much

How do we fix all of these problems? With money. Our commission considered myriad measures to reform the state's death penalty system and recommended several. If all of the reforms we recommended were implemented, the state would reduce the risk of wrongful conviction while still being able to process death penalty cases more quickly.

We currently pay $137 million each year for the state's dysfunctional death penalty. Implementing our recommendations would cost an additional $95 million, for a total price tag of $230 million each

In lieu of the death penalty, many states have made life without parole the maximum sentence.

year. Because it would take many years to increase the pace of review of death penalty cases, we would still need to build a new facility to house the people now on Death Row, at a cost of $400 million.

As Sen. Harmon stated, "California can't afford the dysfunctional death penalty system in place." What he fails to disclose is that California can't afford to fix it either.

Permanent Imprisonment a Better Option

We have an alternative, however. California can and should replace the death penalty with the sentence of permanent imprisonment: life with absolutely no possibility of parole. The past 30 years have shown that permanent imprisonment succeeds where the death penalty fails. It provides severe and certain punishment, ensuring that dangerous people are off the streets. It also provides peace of mind and finality to the family of murder victims, while the death penalty drags them through decades of painful appeals. And, it would save the state hundreds of millions of dollars a year.

It is time for the voters to fix this system: We should replace the death penalty with permanent imprisonment.

EVALUATING THE AUTHORS' ARGUMENTS:

Jon Streeter, Bill Hing, and Diane Bellas suggest that sentencing a murderer to life in prison without parole ensures that the murderer will never again be able to take a life. How do you think Debra J. Saunders, author of the following viewpoint, might respond to this idea?

Life in Prison Is Not a Good Alternative to the Death Penalty

Debra J. Saunders

"End the death penalty, and these violent con artists could be the first to walk—and it won't be transformative growth for society."

In the following viewpoint Debra J. Saunders warns that life in prison is not a sufficient alternative to the death penalty. She explains that death penalty opponents often say the death penalty should be abolished because society's worst criminals can be sufficiently restrained by a sentence of life in prison without parole (LWOP). But Saunders warns that if the death penalty is abolished, LWOP will be abolitionists' next target. To prove her point, she cites evidence from anti-death-penalty groups who claim that LWOP is unnecessary and unfair to criminals. Saunders warns that abolishing the death penalty will lead to the abolition of LWOP, which is a last line of defense that keeps society's worst criminals from being released from jail. Saunders concludes that life in prison is not an adequate punishment

for murders, and the death penalty is needed to permanently inca-
pacitate them.

Saunders is a conservative columnist whose articles have appeared
in the *San Francisco Chronicle*, the *Wall Street Journal*, the *Weekly Standard*, and other publications.

AS YOU READ, CONSIDER THE FOLLOWING QUESTIONS:
1. What is the Sentencing Project and what is its goal, according to
   Saunders?
2. In Saunders's opinion, where should criminals atone for their
   crimes?
3. Who is Kevin Cooper and how does he factor into the author's
   argument?

Because courts can sentence murderers to life without parole,
why not get rid of the death penalty? It's a frequent question
posed by readers and advocates who oppose the death penalty.
For years, my answer has been: If death-penalty opponents ever suc-
ceed in eliminating capital punishment, their next target for elimination will be life without parole—or as lawyers call it, LWOP.

As if to prove my point, the Sentencing Project just released a report, "No Exit: The Expanding Use of Life Sentences in America,"
which advocated for—you guessed it—the elimination of LWOP.
The report also lamented that governors and parole boards are not
paroling more prisoners serving life (with parole) sentences.

A Last Line of Defense
The death penalty still stands, and already opponents are trying to
shave the only alternative sentence that ostensibly protects the general public from the most dangerous predators.

(I say ostensibly in view of the fact that California's last lethal-injection
recipient, Clarence Ray Allen, chose to aid his legal appeal by ordering the
murder of eight witnesses while he served a life sentence in prison for
murder. An accomplice killed three innocent people before he was caught.)

The Sentencing Project is a national organization that works to
promote alternatives to incarceration. Ashley Nellis, one of the authors,

Murderers Who Have Killed Again

Supporters of the death penalty argue that unless murderers are permanently incapacitated by death, they will go on to kill again. Convicted murders kill inmates and prison guards; kill people after they escape from prison; or kill people after they are paroled. Some killers who have continued to murder after they were convicted include:

California
John Miller—convicted of murdering an infant in 1958. Upon his parole in 1975, he killed his parents.

Florida
Donald Dillbeck—imprisoned for the murder of a policeman in 1979. Escaped from prison in 1990, upon which he killed a woman.

Texas
Benny Lee Chaffin—convicted of murder in Texas but not executed. After being paroled he kidnapped, raped, and murdered a 9-year-old girl.

Oregon
Dwain Little—received a life sentence in 1966 for the rape and murder of a 16-year-old girl. After he was released in 1977, he shot a family of four.

Missouri
Charles Crawford—paroled in 1990 for a 1965 murder. In 1994 he killed again.

Illinois
David E. Maust—Upon his release for the murder of a 15-year-old boy, he killed three teenagers.

Oklahoma
Zeno E. Sims—Upon his release from prison after serving 8 years for the murder of a 24-year-old man, he murdered a 15-year-old girl.

Nevada
Arthur J. Bomar, Jr.—was released from prison after serving 11 years of a murder sentence, only to rape and murder George Mason University star athlete Aimee Willard.

Utah
Jack Henry Abbott—murdered a fellow prison inmate but was released early from prison. Six weeks later he fatally stabbed actor Richard Adan.

Virginia
Dawud Mu'Min—escaped from prison in 1988 while serving time for the murder of a cab driver. Shortly after his escape he raped and killed a woman. He was executed in 1997.

Alabama
Cuhuatemoc Hinricky Peraita—murdered a fellow inmate while serving a sentence of life without parole for 3 other murders.

Mississippi
Jimmy Lee Gray—After being released for the murder of a 16-year-old girl, he kidnapped, sodomized, and suffocated a three-year-old girl.

Pennsylvania
Philadelphia Industrial Correctional Center—in 1994, an inmate who was already serving time for murder stabbed three prison guards.

Taken from: Wesley Lowe, Pro Capital Punishment Page, July 22, 2009. www.wesleylowe.com/cp.html.com.

told me that the Sentencing Project opposes both the death penalty and LWOP.

She is aware that getting rid of LWOP would remove a common argument in favor of ending capital punishment. But: "Both of those sentences are problematic because they offer no hope for release—and basically say that certain people are unredeemable. They have no incentive to try to turn their lives around."

People Sentenced to LWOP or Death Are Dangerous

Clearly there is a schism between how the Sentencing Project and your average juror looks at felony murder. Juries sentence violent criminals to death or life behind bars because they see certain crimes as so brutal that they must be punished severely. The 48-page report addressed LWOP and the fact that "it has become increasingly difficult for persons serving a life sentence to be released on parole." It lamented the fact that governors are decreasingly likely to heed parole board recommendations to release convicts and unabashedly called for an end to juvenile LWOP sentences.

The problem is: I can't trust a report with five tables dissecting the racial and ethnic makeup of inmates —48 percent are black, 33 percent are white and 14 are Latino—but not a single chart that tells me what exactly America's 140,000-plus inmates did to earn their life sentences. Nellis and co-author Ryan S. King think it is wrong that one in 11 prisoners is serving a sentence of life or LWOP, but they don't provide information that indicates whether one of 11 inmates is seriously dangerous and belongs behind bars. "We didn't have access to the crimes that were committed," Nellis told me, although she conceded "most" inmates serving LWOP sentences "are in for murder."

> **FAST FACT**
>
> In 1978, Clarence Ray Allen was sentenced to life in prison without possibility of parole. From prison, he arranged to have three people who testified against him murdered. Allen was finally executed in 2006.

In that the Sentencing Project has had no problem coming up with statistics on draconian sentences that reveal the undeniable and outrageous excesses of America's war on drugs, I don't think the researchers tried too hard. When the statistics bolster their argument, they find them.

Criminals Should Repent—from Within Their Cells

Don't worry about the [serial killer] Charlie Mansons of the world, Nellis told me, as they never will be paroled. And she stressed this important point: "We don't believe that everyone should get parole. We think everyone should have the opportunity for parole."

As the report argued, "Life-without-parole sentences are costly, shortsighted and ignore the potential for transformative personal growth."

This may surprise some readers (as they know I believe in the death penalty), but I do not believe the criminal justice system should rob the repentant of the opportunity for transformative personal growth. I believe convicted killers can atone—but they should do so from within their prison cells.

And they can repent on Death Row. "No Exit" cites the American Law Institute's support for "elimination of life without parole as an alternative to the death penalty." But it's clear advocates don't want an alternative.

Given their objections to life sentences, if California or the federal government ever discards the death penalty, all the money that gets sucked into fueling bogus death-penalty appeals simply will move to bankroll anti-LWOP appeals.

To the extent that appeals might help an innocent prisoner, that would be fine. But if you follow these issues, you know that the most unrepentant sociopaths will exploit any opening.

We Need the Death Penalty to Keep Us Safe

Think Kevin Cooper, who killed chiropractors Doug and Peggy Ryen, their 10-year-old daughter and an 11-year-old houseguest in 1983 after he escaped from the California Institution for Men at Chino, where he was serving time under a phony name for burglary. DNA evidence has proved Cooper's guilt—yet from Death Row, he still finds lawyers who will ignore the evidence, change Cooper's story and assert that he is not guilty.

Think convicted cop-killer Mumia Abu Jamal,—who was shot in the chest by Philadelphia police Officer Daniel Faulkner—and found

Protesters in support of convicted cop-killer Mumia Abu Jamal rally outside a federal court-house in Philadelphia, Pennsylvania, on May 17, 2007. Mumia is considered a political prisoner by his supporters, who say the district attorney deliberately kept African Americans off the jury in his trial.

at the crime scene with the gun and identified by four eyewitnesses as Faulkner's killer. To this day, supporters argue that he is a "political prisoner."

End the death penalty, and these violent con artists could be the first to walk—and it won't be transformative growth for society.

Chapter 2

Is the Death Penalty Just?

Shown here is the death chamber at San Quentin Prison in California. Many people believe that execution by lethal gas constitutes cruel and unusual punishment.

The Death Penalty Delivers Justice

Mark Davis

> *"The death penalty rests on the strong foundation of its symmetry and rightness."*

In the following viewpoint Mark Davis argues that the death penalty is just. He describes how watching an execution turned him into an ardent supporter of capital punishment. In watching a murderer be killed for his crime, he witnessed how it offered the victim's family members closure and justice—as one witness put it, it did not seem just to let his father's murderer live out his life in prison, reading novels in the exercise yard or eating in the prison cafeteria. For him, death was the only true justice that could be delivered, short of bringing his father back. Davis acknowledges that the death penalty has problems, but argues these should be fixed rather than abolishing the death penalty because of its flaws. He concludes that the death penalty offers victims and criminals the justice they deserve.

Davis is a columnist for the *Dallas Morning News*. His radio show, *The Mark Davis Show*, is heard weekdays nationwide on the ABC Radio Network.

Mark Davis, "Fix Death Penalty with Scalpel, Not Sledgehammer," RealClearPolitics.com, April 26, 2007. Reproduced by permission of the author.

AS YOU READ, CONSIDER THE FOLLOWING QUESTIONS:
1. What time did the execution witnessed by Davis take place, and what was the method of execution?
2. What does the author mean when he says fixing the death penalty should require a scalpel rather than a sledgehammer?
3. Under what circumstances would Davis agree to reduce the number of executions performed?

B efore July 1984, I had been fairly ambivalent about the death penalty. It never bothered me that we executed murderers, but nor did I yearn for executions as the only proper way to dispense justice to killers.

A reporter stands in the witness area of the execution room at the Maryland State Penitentiary. A prison employee operates a curtain that will be drawn back so that witnesses may watch the execution.

At 26, I had been a grownup for only a few years, still negotiating the various forks in the road that would lead to my eventual political stances. But on one summer morning 23 years ago, I became a staunch supporter of the death penalty, and I have not wavered since.

It was the day I witnessed an execution.

A Life-Changing Experience

As the news director of a Jacksonville radio station, my name came up on the rotating list of media witnesses welcomed to the Florida State Prison for each execution.

Death penalty opponents had long argued for televising executions, presuming the public would share their revulsion. I thus approached the event with a certain anxiety; Florida had not joined the ranks of the states employing the sleepy drabness of lethal injection. This was to be an inmate's appointment with Old Sparky, the electric chair Florida had used since 1924.

Just before 7 a.m., the blinds on our witness room window opened, and we saw a multiple murderer strapped into the chair. Moments later, 2,000 volts of electricity coursed through his body. It is less visually spectacular than one might think—thick straps kept convulsions to a minimum, and a thick rubber veil hid the face of the condemned.

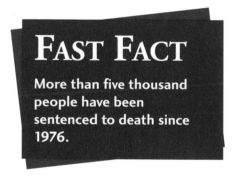

FAST FACT

More than five thousand people have been sentenced to death since 1976.

But it is still a lot for the mind to absorb, and as we were led out to share details with other media and then ask our own questions of other attendees, I was still processing the entire sensory experience.

Ultimate Justice Delivered

Then I spoke to the victims' family members. From their front row witness seats, they saw the ultimate justice delivered to the man who had brutally killed their loved ones.

They said knowing he was dead would help close their emotional wounds. One told me: "Twenty years from now, as I continue to miss

The Worst Punishment For the Worst Crimes: Capital Offenses by State

Each state allows the death penalty to be given for slightly different crimes. Supporters of the death penalty say execution is a just punishment for murder, rape, terrorism, and other crimes.

State	Offense	State	Offense
Alabama	Intentional murder	Mississippi	Capital murders; aircraft piracy
Arizona	First-degree murder	Missouri	First-degree murder
Arkansas	Capital murder with a finding of at least 1 of 10 aggravating circumstances; treason	Montana	Capital murder with 1 of 9 aggravating circumstances; aggravated sexual intercourse without consent
California	First-degree murder with special circumstances; train wrecking; treason; perjury causing execution	Nebraska	First-degree murder
Colorado	First-degree murder; first-degree kidnapping resulting in death; treason	Nevada	First-degree murder
		New Hampshire	Six categories of capital murder
Connecticut	Capital felony with 8 forms of aggravated homicide	North Carolina	First-degree murder
Delaware	First-degree murder	Ohio	Aggravated murder
Florida	First-degree murder; felony murder; capital drug trafficking; capital sexual battery	Oklahoma	First-degree murder; sex crimes against a child under 14 years of age
Georgia	Murder; kidnapping with bodily injury or ransom when the victim dies; aircraft hijacking; treason	Oregon	Aggravated murder
Idaho	First-degree murder; aggravated kidnapping; perjury resulting in death	Pennsylvania	First-degree murder
		South Carolina	Murder; criminal sexual conduct with a minor
Illinois	First-degree murder	South Dakota	First-degree murder
Indiana	Murder	Tennessee	First-degree murder
Kansas	Capital murder	Texas	Criminal homicide
Kentucky	Murder with aggravating factors; kidnapping with aggravating factors	Utah	Aggravated murder
Louisiana	First-degree murder; aggravated rape of victim under age 13; treason	Virginia	First-degree murder
		Washington	Aggravated first-degree murder
Maryland	First-degree murder, either premeditated or during the commission of a felony, provided that certain death eligibility requirements are satisfied	Wyoming	First-degree murder

Taken from: National Prisoner Statistics Program (NPS-8), Bureau of Justice Statistics, December 17, 2007.

holidays, birthdays, every day with my father, I don't want to think of him eating cafeteria meals and reading novels in the exercise yard."

And a death penalty supporter was born.

Death Penalty Problems Should Be Fixed

I know full well that we can deliver a very harsh punishment through the promise of life without the hope of parole. For some murderers, there may be a mitigating circumstance that makes that the appropriate sentence.

I also know the death penalty in America is the product of a flawed human system. As the ranks grow of inmates released through DNA evidence by the Innocence Project legal clinics, all of us should wonder: Have we ever executed an innocent person?

I would think we almost certainly have, and as a death penalty supporter, I believe I have a special responsibility to adhere to a venerable standard: Better the guilty go free than one innocent man die.

The solution to this is not to scrap the entirety of a capital punishment system that is overwhelmingly just and popular in Texas and around the country. The death penalty issues in each state require scalpels, not sledgehammers.

The Justice Everyone Deserves

While we convict people of various crimes based on a standard of surpassing reasonable doubt, I am thoroughly satisfied with reserving the death penalty for those killers who have acted beyond the shadow of a doubt—stories of confession, uncontested witnesses, surveillance video and the like. I will gladly reduce the number of executions to help achieve the goal of certainty in the cases when we do deliver the ultimate punishment.

I don't know if the death penalty is a deterrent, and I don't care. The death penalty rests on the strong foundation of its symmetry and rightness. If that foundation has eroded due to a tiny percentage of cases of human failing, let those be addressed and corrected. We should not succumb to the urge to overreact, sacrificing a just practice that affords both killers and victims the justice they deserve.

EVALUATING THE AUTHORS' ARGUMENTS:

Both this viewpoint by Mark Davis and the following one by Elizabeth Morgan feature the stories of murder victims' family members. The family members in this viewpoint say the death penalty offered them justice and closure; the family members in the following viewpoint think differently. In your opinion, how is it that people who have both lost loved ones to murder could react so differently to the death penalty? Explain the factors that might cause grieving people to hold differing opinions on the justness of the death penalty.

Viewpoint

2

The Death Penalty Does Not Deliver Justice

Elizabeth Morgan

"There are some injustices that human law cannot reconcile— and ought not try to reconcile."

In the following viewpoint Elizabeth Morgan argues that the death penalty has many serious problems and seems to run counter to the Christian teaching about forgiveness. Morgan's resolve on this issue was tested when her niece was murdered and the perpetrator was caught. In the course of personally experiencing such horrific events, Morgan did not find that the prospect of the death penalty for the murderer offered her the hope of justice or peace. Rather Morgan found that the memorial service filled with scripture, forgiveness, the comfort of friends, and remembering the good of the life that was taken helped her more than seeking the death penalty for her niece's assailant.

Elizabeth Morgan teaches English at Eastern University in St. Davids, Pennsylvania.

Elizabeth Morgan, "Crime and Punishment: Wrestling with the Death Penalty (Book Review)," *The Christian Century*, vol. 123, no. 20, October 3, 2006, pp. 30–33. Copyright © 2006 The Christian Century Foundation. Reproduced by permission from *The Christian Century*.

AS YOU READ, CONSIDER THE FOLLOWING QUESTIONS:
1. What reasons does Morgan give for why she had been against the death penalty before she experienced the tragedy of murder in her own life?
2. What sort of criminal past did the assailant in the story have?
3. What sentence did Morgan's niece's murderer receive?

E veryone has an opinion about the death penalty. Theoretically (and abstractly) I have always been opposed to it, for the usual reasons: there are too many mistakes for such a permanent solution; there are too many racial, IQ and class inequities; there is no conclusive evidence that the death penalty deters violent crime—and there is a good bit of evidence that it *is* violent crime. Also, it seems to me as a Christian that it contradicts the gospel call for forgiveness and truncates the possibility of transformation.

I've never been able to forget a story I heard on public radio told by a man called Race Horse. Having been evangelized by no one, Race Horse found himself in the worst conditions of solitary confinement— "the hole" in a southern prison. It was dark, the guards had taken his clothes, he was defenseless. Inexplicably and quite suddenly, he was caught up in the assurance that God loved him, and his life was never the same.

But all of these fine sentiments about capital punishment were tested eight years ago when my 25-year-old niece was brutally murdered, along with two young coworkers, in a Starbucks in the upscale Georgetown community of Washington, D.C. It was the end of a Fourth of July weekend, there was an accumulation of money in the safe, and Cait was the manager in charge of clean-up. An assailant with two firearms entered the coffee shop and killed all three of them without taking a penny. Cait died from three gunshot wounds to the head and chest, with the keys to the safe clutched in her hand. The Starbucks manual expressly tells employees not to use heroic measures in the face of violent crime, but certain young people will ever be brave. Because it was Georgetown, because there were three victims, news clips of the three body bags being removed from the scene played on TV over and over again.

The National Coalition to Abolish the Death Penalty brings together many different groups that oppose the death penalty.

The search for the assailant went on for a year and a half. The FBI became involved because the prime suspect had committed several violent crimes—he had killed a security guard and wounded a Prince George's County police officer—and because he was involved in interstate drug running. The District of Columbia does not have capital punishment; the feds do. When Janet Reno called for the death penalty, we had to face facts; we were a divided family. My mother,

Unjustly Incarcerated

Since the death penalty was reinstated in 1976, at least 118 people on death row have been exonerated—or proved innocent. These people spent a combined 1,125 years in prison (each mark represents one of these years). This is one reason death penalty opponents say the system is unjust.

Taken from: Death Penalty Information Center, *Journal of Crime and Criminology, Good Magazine,* September/October 2007. www.good/is.

my sister and I continued to stand firmly against capital punishment; others were less sure. Luckily the assailant, Carl Cooper, took a plea bargain and confessed to enough crimes to get him life in prison without parole. But all of this caused me to become much clearer in my own reasoning.

What do families expect to glean from execution? Closure? Some books cannot be closed. Cait's could not. The arrest brought great relief, but we don't want closure on her life or even her death, for the way she died tells us a great deal about the world we live in and the kind of work that needs to be done to make all of our neighborhoods safer places to live.

Justice? What was done to Cait and Emory and Aaron was grossly unjust. Killing Carl Cooper would not take that away. Killing everyone on death row would not take that away. It is an affront that will remain on the record until all injustice is wiped away by divine intervention. There are some injustices that human law cannot reconcile—and ought not try to reconcile.

Peace? If we had waited until Cooper's trial and ultimate execution for our peace, we would be troubled people indeed. In such a rending of life and family, peace needs to be imminent, continually sought, recognized in small acts. Planning the memorial service, filled with poetry and scripture, meant much to me. At the service itself, during the last hymn, "Amazing Grace," people spontaneously moved into the aisles so they could hold one another—and hold on. Witnessing Cooper's execution would have been cold comfort indeed compared with these events.

I later received a letter from my sister in which she reflected on the memorial service for Cait. She said: "I can only think on it with pleasure: turning destructive hate/venom into love and forgiveness, good memories of this essentially good child. There's no doubt that I think Carl Cooper—having admitted to at least five murders— should be imprisoned. I have no idea how to redeem him, to correct his hurts and terrible passions, nor do I have much hope for that—though as I think about it, I may try to visit him someday."

That is my story. We need stories because they humanize the abstract and allow both teller and hearers to locate themselves within a shifting landscape of moral values.

EVALUATING THE AUTHOR'S ARGUMENTS:

Elizabeth Morgan bases her opposition to the death penalty on the fact that she has lost a loved one to murder. If a loved one of yours were murdered, how do you think you would feel about the death penalty? Would you feel that justice would be served by seeing your loved one's murderer executed? Or would you feel that an execution would dishonor the memory of your loved one? Explain your reasoning.

Execution by Lethal Injection Is Too Humane

Dave Gibson

> *"The method of lethal injection is in fact much too easy for these monsters."*

In the following viewpoint Dave Gibson argues that executing condemned prisoners by lethal injection is too humane a method for such criminals. He discusses how death penalty opponents have tried to abolish lethal injection (the process of executing a person by giving them a fatal cocktail of drugs) by arguing that the process causes prisoners undue pain and is thus inhumane. But Gibson argues that lethal injection offers prisoners a peaceful, painless death, which in his opinion is far better than they deserve. Considering that murderers cared not for their victims' comfort at their time of death, Gibson thinks it is wrong for death penalty opponents to give any thought to the comfort of murderers—in his opinion, they forfeited this right when they committed the worst crimes known to man. Gibson concludes that lethal injection is a humane form of execution and the death penalty a just process—but even if it were not, Gibson says, that would be acceptable for murderers.

Gibson has worked in the security industry for many years and has written about the death penalty and other topics for the *Washington Times* and the *Norfolk (VA) Crime Examiner*.

AS YOU READ, CONSIDER THE FOLLOWING QUESTIONS:
1. How much does the author say was the value of the two gold necklaces for which Carlos Garza was killed?
2. What is the three-drug process used in lethal injection executions, as described by Gibson?
3. Who is Barbara Christian, and how does she factor into the author's argument?

A little before 7:00 p.m. tonight, Texas death row inmate Reginald Blanton will be escorted from a holding cell in the East Building of the Huntsville Unit, and taken into a room and strapped to a gurney, where he will be given a combination of drugs which will put him to sleep and then stop his heart.

Of course, before this execution by lethal injection takes place, Blanton will be allowed a last meal of his choosing and allowed to make a final statement which will be given to the press.

A Brutal Murder
While a last meal and a final statement may not seem like much to a man only minutes away from his execution, they are certainly freedoms which Blanton's victim was denied.

In 2001, a Bexar County jury convicted Blanton for the murder of his friend, Carlos Garza, 22.

On April 4, 2000, Blanton kicked down the door to Garza's apartment, then shot Garza twice in the head, stealing two gold necklaces.

Blanton was later seen on surveillance video selling the jewelry at a local pawn shop for $79.

Murderers Complain About "Undue Pain"
In June 2006, the U.S. Supreme Court ruled that death row inmates could legally challenge the method in which states carry out lethal injections. In *Hill v. Florida*, the inmate claimed that the three drugs used in the execution could possibly cause pain.

The state of Texas executed Reginald Blanton (pictured) for the murder of Carlos Garza in 2001. Garza was killed while being robbed of gold necklaces worth seventy-nine dollars.

The three drug process includes an anesthetic which induces unconsciousness, another which causes paralysis, and the last which stops the heart.

Since the *Hill v. Florida* decision, there have been dozens of suits filed across the country by death row inmates, alleging that their pending lethal injection may possibly cause them undue pain.[1]

---

1. In 2008 the Supreme Court upheld the use of lethal injection in executions, rejecting claims that it caused undue pain.

Why Should Murderers Be Treated Humanely?

On September 26, 2006, a federal judge in San Jose, CA began hearing the case brought forth by convicted murderer Michael Morales. Morales and his lawyers contended that the lethal injection which he was sentenced to receive is actually "cruel and unusual punishment." He was convicted of the 1981 murder of Terri Lynn Winchell of Lodi, CA.

Morales killed the teenaged girl by caving in her skull with a claw hammer.

Morales' attorney Ginger Adams expressed her concerns over the treatment of her murderous client by saying: "The California Department of Corrections and Rehabilitation is institutionally unable to ensure that executions are performed humanely."

One person who was not at all concerned with the humane treatment of Morales, is his victim's mom. Barbara Christian said in a written statement: "As a mother, I don't care what kind of pain Morales feels because of what he did to my daughter. He showed no mercy when she cried out for it. He deserves no mercy."

Lethal Injection Is a Merciful Death

However, by killing Morales through the method of lethal injection, he is likely being shown unwarranted mercy. It is a very serene and apparently rather painless end to the rampage that was his life. In fact, very similar drugs in very similar combinations are used in cases of medically assisted suicide in Oregon, where the practice is legal.

Other methods of killing convicted murderers which have been used in the United States include the firing squad, hanging, the electric chair, and the gas chamber. The method of electrocution can be particularly gruesome. Virginia offers death row inmates the choice of either the electric chair or lethal injection, if the condemned refuses to make a choice, he is then given lethal injection. Since 1995 only one inmate executed in Virginia has chosen the chair.

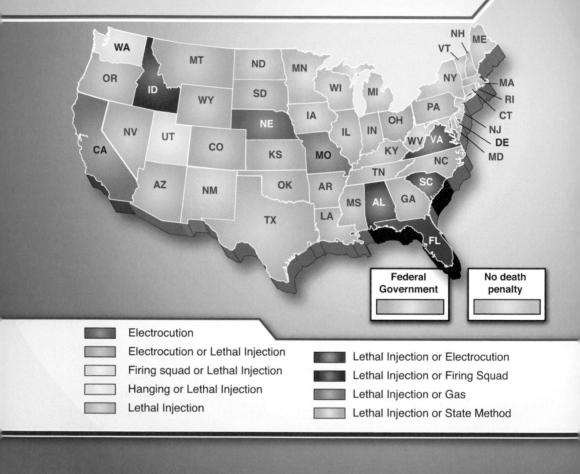

Methods of Execution by State

Of the 35 states that retain the death penalty, most execute via lethal injection, which the Supreme Court has ruled is a humane form of execution that does not cause undue pain to the prisoner.

Federal Government

No death penalty

- Electrocution
- Electrocution or Lethal Injection
- Firing squad or Lethal Injection
- Hanging or Lethal Injection
- Lethal Injection
- Lethal Injection or Electrocution
- Lethal Injection or Firing Squad
- Lethal Injection or Gas
- Lethal Injection or State Method

Taken from: Office of Clark County Prosecuting Attorney, 2009, and Bureau of Justice Statistics.

Executive director Richard Dieter of the Death Penalty Information Center (a group opposed to the use of capital punishment) recently said: "The lethal injection process is unnecessarily painful and risky and that is an Eighth Amendment violation against cruel and unusual punishment."

You see, liberals believe that even the most brutal and bloodthirsty amongst us should never feel any pain, not even a fraction of that which they inflicted upon their innocent victims. As talk show host

Michael Savage claims: "Liberalism is a mental disorder!" . . . It must be, it is the only way to explain how anyone could spend their energy attempting to secure a pain-free and compassionate end to the life of a rapist-murderer!

Nothing Wrong with Revenge

The method of lethal injection is in fact much too easy for these monsters. In my opinion, they should either be killed in the same method in which they murdered their victims, or at least given an equally painful and gruesome death such as electrocution or perhaps by being drawn and quartered!

Why is it wrong to inflict pain upon our most savage criminals? . . . There is nothing wrong with a society seeking and gaining some measure of revenge on those who have committed the ultimate crime against our fellow citizens.

It is also an abomination that the same humane method of ending the lives of our beloved and faithful pets is extended to the vermin on death row. Euthanasia for an animal is a decision which is made out of love and compassion for our devoted four-legged friends. Despite what any ACLU [American Civil Liberties Union] lawyer may contend, it is much too good for the human predators now dwelling in this nation's prison system.

Brutal crimes call for brutal consequences—Not sedatives!

EVALUATING THE AUTHOR'S ARGUMENTS:

Dave Gibson thinks it is inappropriate to care about the comfort of a murderer as he is about to be executed. Do you agree? Why or why not? What value, if any, do you see in caring about whether a murderer is executed humanely —and is a "humane execution" even possible? Base your opinion on evidence from the texts you have read.

Execution by Lethal Injection Is Not Humane

Human Rights Watch

"Prisoners in the United States are executed by means that the American Veterinary Medical Association regards as too cruel to use on dogs and cats."

Human Rights Watch is an international non-governmental organization dedicated to the protection of human rights around the world. In the following report, it argues that execution by lethal injection is not humane. It says that although lethal injection appears from the outside to be a painless, peaceful way to die, in reality, prisoners experience excruciating pain and suffering during the procedure. The drugs that cause death are often administered incorrectly or in such a way that the prisoners are awake enough to feel their organs becoming paralyzed. Though prisoners cannot scream out, Human Rights Watch says the agony they feel upon their death is real, terrible, and unnecessary. Furthermore, lethal injections are frequently botched, causing a prisoner's death to be physically and emotionally drawn out. For all of these reasons the author concludes that the use of lethal injection in American executions is inhumane and must be stopped immediately.

Human Rights Watch, *So Long as They Die: Lethal Injections in the United States*, New York, NY: Human Rights Watch, 2006. Reproduced by permission.

AS YOU READ, CONSIDER THE FOLLOWING QUESTIONS:
  1. How many death penalty states does the author say have adopted lethal injection?
  2. What is pancuronium bromide and what does Human Rights Watch say it does to the body?
  3. What does the author say happened in six lethal injection executions in California?

Compared to electrocution, lethal gas, or hanging, death by lethal injection appears painless and humane, perhaps because it mimics a medical procedure. More palatable to the general public, lethal injection has become the most prevalent form of execution in the United States. Thirty-seven of the thirty-eight death penalty states and the federal government have adopted it; for nineteen states, it is the only legal method of execution.

Prisoners Experience Excruciating Pain

In the standard method of lethal injection used in the United States, the prisoner lies strapped to a gurney, a catheter with an intravenous line attached is inserted into his vein, and three drugs are injected into the line by executioners hidden behind a wall. The first drug is an anesthetic (sodium thiopental), followed by a paralytic agent (pancuronium bromide), and, finally, a drug that causes the heart to stop beating (potassium chloride).

Although supporters of lethal injection believe the prisoner dies painlessly, there is mounting evidence that prisoners may have experienced excruciating pain during their executions. This should not be surprising given that corrections agencies have not taken the steps necessary to ensure a painless execution. They use a sequence of drugs and a method of administration that were created with minimal expertise and little deliberation three decades ago, and that were then adopted unquestioningly by state officials with no medical or scientific background. Little has changed since then. As a result, prisoners in the United States are executed by means that the American Veterinary Medical Association regards as too cruel to use on dogs and cats.

Kenneth Roth (pictured) is the executive director of Human Rights Watch. The international organization works to end the death penalty worldwide.

Human Rights Watch opposes capital punishment in all circumstances. But until the thirty-eight death penalty states and the federal government abolish the death penalty, international human rights law requires them to use execution methods that will produce the least possible physical and mental suffering. It is not enough for public officials to believe that lethal injection is inherently more humane than the electric chair. States must choose carefully among possible drugs and administration procedures to be sure they have developed the specific protocol that will reduce, to the greatest extent possible, the prisoner's risk of mental or physical agony.

Unsound Procedures Abound

The history of lethal injection executions in the United States reveals no such care on the part of state legislators and corrections officials.

The Death Penalty and International Human Rights Standards

Many universally recognized international treaties have sought to limit or abolish the death penalty even for crimes like genocide.

1948	The United Nations (UN) unanimously adopts the **Universal Declaration of Human Rights**, which proclaims every individual's right to life. It states that no one shall be subjected to cruel or degrading punishment.
1966	The UN adopts the **International Covenant on Civil and Political Rights (ICCPR)**. Article 6 states that "no one shall be arbitrarily deprived of life," and neither pregnant women nor those under 18 at the time of the crime shall receive the death penalty.
1984	The UN General Assembly adopts the **Second Optional Protocol to the ICCPR**, aimed at abolition of the death penalty.
1989	The UN Economic and Social Council (ECOSOC) adopts **Safeguards Guaranteeing Protection of the Rights of Those Facing the Death Penalty.** In the same year, the Safeguards are endorsed by consensus by the UN General Assembly. The Safeguards state that anyone sentenced to death has the right to appeal and to petition for a pardon or commutation and that no one under the age of 18 at the time of the crime shall be put to death.
1990	The **Protocol to the American Convention on Human Rights** is adopted by the General Assembly of the Organization of American States. It provides for the total abolition of the death penalty, allowing for its use in wartime only.
1993	The **International War Crimes Tribunal** does not provide the death penalty as an option, even for the most heinous crimes, such as genocide.
1995	The **UN Convention on the Rights of the Child** comes into force. Article 37(a) prohibits the death penalty for persons under 18 at the time of the crime.
1999	The **UN Commission on Human Rights** (UNCHR) passes a resolution calling on all states that maintain the death penalty to restrict the number of offenses punishable by death.
2002	The Council of Europe's Committee of Ministers adopts **Protocol 13** to the **European Convention on Human Rights**, the first legally binding international treaty to abolish the death penalty in all circumstances, with no exceptions.
2005	The **UNCHR** approves **Human Rights Resolution 2005/59** on the question of the death penalty, calling for all states that still maintain the death penalty to abolish the death penalty completely and, in the meantime, to establish a moratorium on executions.
2007	The **UN General Assembly** approves **Resolution 62/149**, which calls for all states that still maintain the death penalty to establish a moratorium on executions with a view to abolishing the death penalty.

Taken from: Amnesty International USA, November 2008.

The three-drug sequence was developed in 1977 by an Oklahoma medical examiner who had no expertise in pharmacology or anesthesia and who did no research to develop any expertise. Oklahoma's three-drug protocol was copied by Texas, which in 1982 was the first state to execute a man by lethal injection. Texas's sequence was subsequently copied by almost all other states that allow lethal injection executions. Drawing on its own research and that of others, Human Rights Watch has found no evidence that any state seriously investigated whether other drugs or administration methods would be "more humane" than the protocol it adopted.

Corrections agencies continue to display a remarkable lack of due diligence with regard to ascertaining the most "humane" way to kill their prisoners. Even when permitted by statute to consider other drug options, they have not revised their choice of lethal drugs, despite new developments in and knowledge about anesthesia and lethal chemical agents. They continue to use medically unsound procedures to administer the drugs. They have not adopted procedures to make sure the prisoner is in fact deeply unconscious from the anesthesia before the paralyzing second and painful third drugs are administered.

Drugs Cause Paralysis and Asphyxia

Each of the three drugs, in the massive dosages called for in the protocols, is sufficient by itself to cause the death of the prisoner. Within a minute after it enters the prisoner's veins, potassium chloride will cause cardiac arrest. Without proper anesthesia, however, the drug acts as a fire moving through the veins. Potassium chloride is so painful that the American Veterinary Medical Association prohibits its use for euthanasia unless a veterinarian establishes that the animal being killed has been placed by an anesthetic agent at a deep level of unconsciousness (a "surgical plane of anesthesia" marked by non-responsiveness to noxious stimuli).

Pancuronium bromide is a neuromuscular blocking agent that paralyzes voluntary muscles, including the lungs and diaphragm. It would eventually cause asphyxiation of the prisoner. The drug, however, does not affect consciousness or the experience of pain. If the prisoner is not sufficiently anesthetized before being injected with pancuronium bromide, he will feel himself suffocating but be unable to draw a breath—a torturous experience, as anyone knows who has been trapped underwater for even a few seconds. The pancuronium bromide will conceal any agony an insufficiently anesthetized prisoner experiences because of the potassium chloride.

Indeed, the only apparent purpose of the pancuronium bromide is to keep the prisoner still, saving the witnesses and execution team from observing convulsions or other body movements that might occur from the potassium chloride, and saving corrections officials from having to deal with the public relations and legal consequences of a visibly inhumane execution. At least thirty states have banned the use of neuromuscular blocking agents like pancuronium bromide in animal euthanasia because of the danger of undetected, and hence unrelieved, suffering.

Sodium thiopental is the only drug with anesthetic properties used in lethal injections. State protocols specify a dosage of sodium thiopental five to twenty times greater than what would be used in surgery. If this amount of sodium thiopental is administered properly, the prisoner will go limp, stop breathing, and lose consciousness within a minute. The prisoner will not feel the suffocating effects of pancuronium bromide or the agony of potassium chloride. If someone trained to establish and maintain intravenous lines, induce anesthesia, and monitor consciousness were present and involved in the lethal injection execution, the pain the prisoner would feel is the insertion of catheters into his veins. But lethal injection protocols do not include measures to ensure the anesthesia is quickly and effectively administered.

Prisoners' Pain Is Real and Awful

Administering drugs intravenously requires extensive training to ensure that the proper intravenous access is secured with minimal pain, and that it is then maintained. Inserting an intravenous catheter can be particularly difficult when the recipient has veins compromised by drug use—not uncommon among prisoners—and constricted by anxiety. Witnesses have described execution personnel poking repeatedly at prisoners trying to find a good vein. . . .

The risks of pain and suffering faced by prisoners from the current lethal injection protocol are not just hypothetical. There is mounting evidence, including execution records and eyewitness testimony, of botched executions. At least some prisoners may have been insufficiently anesthetized during their executions, experiencing pain but unable to signal their distress, because they were paralyzed. There have been executions where:

- For over an hour, medical technicians and then a physician tried to find a suitable vein for intravenous access. The condemned inmate ended up with one needle in his hand, one in his neck, and a catheter inserted into the vein near his collarbone. One hour and nine minutes after he was strapped to the gurney, the prisoner was pronounced dead.
- A kink in the intravenous tubing stopped some of the drugs from reaching an inmate. In the same execution, the intravenous needle was inserted pointing the wrong way—towards the inmate's fingers instead of his heart, which slowed the effect of the drugs.
- A prisoner who initially lost consciousness during his lethal injection execution began convulsing, opened his eyes, and appeared to be trying to catch his breath while his chest heaved up and down repeatedly. This lasted for approximately ten minutes before his body stopped twitching and thrashing on the gurney.

In six lethal injection executions in California, the condemned inmates' chests were moving up and down several minutes after the administration of the anesthetic, indicating that the inmates may not have been anesthetized deeply enough to avoid experiencing the painful effects of the potassium chloride and that the paralyzing effects of the pancuronium bromide might have prevented them from showing pain. . . .

The Death Penalty Is Inhumane

Human rights law is predicated on recognition of the inherent dignity and the equal and inalienable rights of all people, including even those who have committed terrible crimes. It prohibits torture and other cruel, inhuman or degrading punishment. Human Rights Watch believes these rights cannot be reconciled with the death penalty, a form of punishment unique in its cruelty and finality, and a punishment inevitably and universally plagued with arbitrariness, prejudice, and error.

EVALUATING THE AUTHORS' ARGUMENTS:

Human Rights Watch thinks that lethal injection should be banned because it causes prisoners to suffer unnecessarily. Dave Gibson, author of the previous viewpoint, says lethal injection does not cause prisoners to suffer, but even if it did, convicted murderers deserve a painful death. After reading both viewpoints, with which perspective do you agree, and why? List at least two pieces of evidence that convinced you.

Viewpoint

5

The Death Penalty Violates Human Rights

Connie De La Vega

"The United States, therefore, finds itself at odds on this issue [of capital punishment] with its European counterparts, with its neighbors in the Americas, and with nearly all democracies."

In the following viewpoint Connie De La Vega argues that the United States' use of the death penalty puts it in the company of countries that are known for violating human rights. At the time of writing, the United States still executed people convicted of capital offenses that they committed under the age of eighteen (a practice that was overruled by the Supreme Court in 2005), which most other countries had already abolished. In addition, the United States has failed in several cases to respect the rights that accused internationals are afforded under the Geneva Conventions, such as the right to contact their consulate for assistance. Moreover, in the United States, people awaiting the death penalty are often on death row for years, and the European Court of Human Rights has ruled that keeping people on death row for so long is a violation of the human right not to be

Connie De La Vega, "Going It Alone: The Rest of the Civilized World Has Abolished the Death Penalty. Will the United States Follow Suit?" *The American Prospect*, vol. 15, no. 7, 2004, pp. A22ff. Copyright © 2004 The American Prospect, Inc. Reproduced by permission from *The American Prospect*, 11 Beacon Street, Suite 1120, Boston, MA 02108.

subject to inhuman and degrading treatment. Finally, De La Vega argues that America's use of the death penalty has jeopardized its relationships with some of its closest allies and embarrassed it in international courts. For all of these reasons De La Vega concludes that the United States' use of the death penalty violates international standards of human rights and must be abolished.

AS YOU READ, CONSIDER THE FOLLOWING QUESTIONS:
1. What did the Commission on Human Rights do in 2001?
2. What did the Inter-American Commission on Human Rights do in 2003?
3. What did the Oklahoma Court of Criminal Appeals do in the case of Osbaldo Torres, and why?

As you have read in the preceding pages, a large majority of countries in the world have abolished the death penalty. In order to join the European Union, for example, countries have to become parties to the European Convention for the Protection of Human Rights and Fundamental Freedoms, and specifically to Protocol 6, which explicitly abolishes the death penalty. Thus, capital punishment has been eradicated in all of western Europe and most of eastern and central Europe. Most of the countries of the Americas have also abolished the death penalty. Indeed, it was repealed in South Africa after the end of apartheid, where it clearly had been one of the tools of repression used by whites against the black majority. (Countries still using the death penalty include China, Japan, and many Muslim nations.)

The United States, therefore, finds itself at odds on this issue with its European counterparts, with its neighbors in the Americas, and with nearly all democracies—a great many of the countries it has traditionally allied itself with on addressing human-rights problems globally. This failure to follow the trend toward abolition has begun to affect America's influence in the international arena.

Nowhere is this clearer than with respect to the execution of persons who committed their crimes when they were under the age of 18. The United States is arguably the sole violator of the international prohibition of such executions. Numerous treaties and pronouncements by international bodies denounce the practice. Of the six countries besides the United States where juveniles have been executed since 1990—Congo, Iran, Nigeria, Pakistan, Saudi Arabia, and Yemen—the laws recently have been changed or the governments have denied that executions continue to take place. Amnesty International reported that a juvenile offender was executed in China in 2003, but allegedly there had been problems verifying his age. China raised its death-penalty eligibility age to 18 in 1997. And in Iran, the parliament passed a bill in December of 2003 removing the provisions for executions of juveniles. If Iran's Guardian Council ratifies the measure, as many predict, the United States will achieve a highly dubious distinction as the world's only country to openly execute juvenile offenders.

FAST FACT

America's use of the death penalty puts it in the company of well-known human rights abusers such as Sudan, North Korea, and Saudi Arabia and in opposition to its allies and human rights champions such as France, Germany, and the United Kingdom.

That fact continues to embarrass the United States at the international level. It was one of half a dozen countries specifically named as a violator in a resolution passed in 1999 by the United Nations Sub-Commission on Promotion and Protection of Human Rights. The United States was singled out as the country that accounted for 10 of the 19 juvenile executions occurring in the preceding 10 years. It may be the only time that this nation was mentioned in any human rights resolution by a body of the United Nations. Perhaps still more embarrassing was an attempt last year by the United States to delete language condemning the execution of juvenile offenders from a resolution on the Rights of the Child supported by the UN Commission on Human Rights. The effort to strip the language failed by a vote of 51-to-1 (with the United States the lone dissenter), and prompted sharp criticism from several commission members, among them close U.S. allies in Europe and Latin America.

Other events suggest that the United States will increasingly be called to task for its own failure to implement human-rights norms, especially in relation to the death penalty. In 2001, the United States was voted off the Commission on Human Rights for the first time in that body's 54-year history. That action may be blamed on many factors, but America's record on the death penalty was at least one point of contention among the nations that failed to support America's renewal.

Similarly, our nation's embrace of the death penalty has jeopardized our status at the Council of Europe, a political organization representing 45 nations across the European continent. In 2001, the council's parliamentary assembly passed a resolution requiring Japan and the United States to impose an immediate moratorium on executions and to take steps to abolish the death penalty in order to maintain their nonvoting observer status. In 2003, the Inter-American Commission on Human Rights, the main human-rights body of the Organization of American States, rejected the sole U.S. candidate for membership, leaving the United States without a seat on the seven-member commission for the first time since it was created in 1959. That vote, too, has been blamed on a number of factors, but it surely hasn't helped that the United States had several commission decisions issued against it with respect to the juvenile death penalty, and has refused to take any steps to implement them.

International adjudicatory bodies are increasingly rendering decisions against the United States with regard to other violations of international treaties and standards related to the death penalty. Most recently, the International Court of Justice (ICJ) has issued opinions that the United States is bound by the provisions of the Vienna Convention on Consular Relations in cases brought against the United States by several of its allies. That treaty provides that persons arrested in a foreign country are supposed to be notified about their right to contact their consulate for assistance. In the wake of repeated violations of the treaty by a number of U.S. states, Paraguay, Germany, and Mexico brought claims against the United States on behalf of their nationals on death row here. The order by the ICJ in the case brought by Mexico affects more than 50 Mexican citizens, 31 of whom are on California's death row at San Quentin.

Prior to the ICJ case, the Inter-American Court on Human Rights had issued an advisory opinion regarding the application of the Vienna

Convention to death-penalty cases. Interestingly, the first court to address the ICJ opinion regarding the condemned Mexican nationals was the Oklahoma Court of Criminal Appeals, that state's highest court for criminal matters. Basing its ruling on the ICJ opinion, the appeals court in May ordered a new hearing for Osbaldo Torres, a Mexican convicted of the 1993 murder of an Oklahoma couple during a burglary of their home. Within a few hours of the ruling, the governor commuted Torres' sentence to life without parole, referring to the United States' obligations under the Vienna Convention and the fact that the State Department had urged him to consider that commitment. As this case demonstrates, the federal government does—and must—play a role in urging the states to comply with U.S. treaty obligations.

Individuals charged with capital crimes have also been using international forums to fight their extraditions to the United States. In one case, a young German national named Jens Soering was accused of murdering his girlfriend's parents in Virginia. After he was arrested in England, the U.S. government requested his extradition to stand trial for the killings, for which he faced the possibility of the death penalty. The European Court of Human Rights ruled that prolonged detention on death row violates the prohibition against inhuman and degrading treatment, and that the United Kingdom would violate the European Convention if it extradited Soering to Virginia because he would suffer from what it termed the "death-row phenomenon." Eventually, Soering was extradited—but only after Virginia agreed not to seek capital punishment in his case.

To date, the U.S. Supreme Court has refused to grant certiorari in other cases that have invoked the death row phenomenon—shorthand for the mental anguish that persons awaiting execution suffer from—despite the various international bodies that have ruled it to be a human-rights violation. Perhaps it is cause for some optimism, at least, that justices John Paul Stevens and Stephen Breyer, in the more recent case of Texas death-row inmate Clarence Lackey, wrote that state and federal courts should study whether long execution delays could constitute "cruel and unusual punishment" in violation of the Eighth Amendment.

In another extradition case, Charles Chitat Ng, a former U.S. Marine wanted for a string of grisly murders in California, fought his ex-

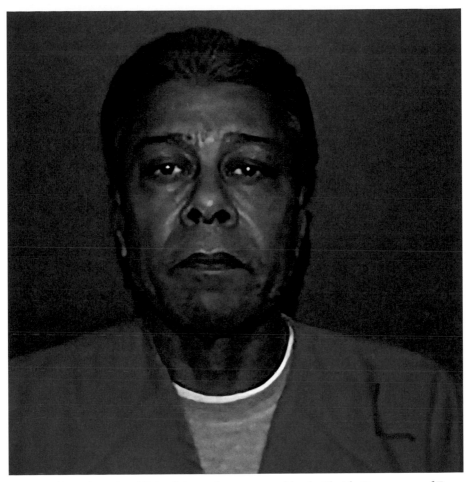

Convicted murderer Angel Diaz (pictured) was executed by the Florida Department of Executions in 2006. Witnesses say he grimaced in pain for thirty-four minutes before dying, but because of the lethal drugs in his body he was unable to speak. Many consider this method of execution to be cruel and unusual punishment and a violation of human rights.

tradition from Canada on the grounds that he faced execution by asphyxiation—a punishment, he argued, that would violate his rights under the International Covenant on Civil and Political Rights (ICCPR). He filed a complaint against Canada before the Human Rights Committee, the body that oversees enforcement of the ICCPR. The committee found that execution by gas asphyxiation would indeed result in prolonged suffering, constituting cruel and inhuman treatment in violation of the ICCPR, and that Canada had violated the treaty by permitting Ng's extradition. (The 9th U.S. Circuit Court of Appeals subsequently upheld a lower court's ruling that execution by gas asphyxiation violates the Eighth Amendment.) Since that decision, Canada has developed its own jurisprudence on this topic. Along with the European countries, it now also refuses to extradite persons who may be subject to the death penalty in the United States following an opinion by its supreme court based on its own constitutional guarantees of the right to life and liberty.

As these examples illustrate, other countries seem increasingly willing to find ways to pressure the United States with respect to its continued use of the death penalty. Moreover, America's efforts to combat terrorism will be made more difficult because friendly countries will not extradite suspects if they face the death penalty. Together, they point to an inescapable conclusion: If the United States wants to regain its role as promoter and protector of human rights around the world, it first needs to address its own violations of internationally recognized standards.

EVALUATING THE AUTHORS' ARGUMENTS:

Compare this viewpoint by Connie De La Vega with the following one by Tyler Trumbach, in which he argues that the death penalty does not violate human rights. Which viewpoint makes a more compelling argument? Support your view with evidence from each viewpoint.

Viewpoint

6

The Death Penalty Does Not Violate Human Rights

Tyler Trumbach

"This country only issues the death penalty by means of due process. Therefore, no human rights are violated."

Tyler Trumbach was a student at Columbia University when he wrote the following viewpoint, which argues that the death penalty docs not violate human rights. Trumbach agrees that all citizens, even murderers, have a right to life and liberty. But he points out that the Fourteenth Amendment says that a citizen's rights can be curtailed if, after due process of law, they are found guilty of a crime. Trumbach thinks the justice system affords murderers due process, which is the responsibility of the government to grant to its citizens the legal rights to which they are entitled. In Trumbach's opinion, death row prisoners forfeited their right to life and liberty when they murdered their victims—victims are the ones who truly have their rights violated. He concludes that the death penalty does not violate human rights, because murderers are fairly tried and punished under the law for heinous crimes that deserve severe punishment.

AS YOU READ, CONSIDER THE FOLLOWING QUESTIONS:
1. Why does the author not consider the death penalty to be "stooping to the murderer's level"?
2. Why does Trumbach not care whether or not the death penalty deters murder?
3. What two suggestions does the author make for fixing the death penalty?

There are few issues more contentious than the death penalty. While other democratic nations have abolished and condemned the death penalty, the United States is one of the last to still carry out capital punishment. In spite of this fact, I believe the use of the death penalty in the U.S. can be justified in cases of murder. Capital punishment does not violate human rights and is an essential part of any judicial system.

What About a Victim's Right?

I imagine that I am taking a very unpopular position among the student body at Columbia University. Therefore, to prevent any misunderstanding or animosity, I feel it necessary that I state that my beliefs have nothing to do with the political party I happen to affiliate with. I came to support capital punishment after studying the issue and looking at the facts. I also feel that I must state that while I support the principle of the death penalty, I still hold some reservations on its implementation in the United States. In order to better understand my beliefs on the issue of capital punishment, I think it necessary to clarify some misconceptions about the death penalty.

First of all, it must be understood that the death penalty does not violate human rights. It seems funny to me that those against the death penalty will ardently fight for the human rights of a murderer while ignoring the rights of a victim. Doesn't a victim have a right to life that was infringed upon by a murderer? The U.S. Constitution guarantees many rights. It is understood that the rights to prosecute are given to the state when the law is broken. After all, there is no outcry when citizens are incarcerated for robbery. Is this not a violation of

Pro-death-penalty advocates point to the rights of murdered victims as being reason enough to sentence murderers to death.

their right to liberty? No, it is understood that the state had the right to take away their right to liberty after they committed a crime. Even the Fourteenth Amendment states that the right to life, liberty, or property can be withheld after due process of the law. This country only issues the death penalty by means of due process. Therefore no human rights are violated.

Justice, Not Revenge

Secondly, the death penalty is not a form of revenge—it is a form of justice. If the death penalty is simply a form of legalized murder used to exact vengeance on a murderer, then life imprisonment is a form of legalized kidnapping. We are not "stooping to the murderer's level" by carrying out the death penalty because the murderer is receiving due process for his crimes (something, I would like to add, they denied their victim). The execution of a murderer follows a trial and appellate review. It is not a form of revenge, but rather a form of justice.

The Purpose of Punishment

Finally, it must be understood that the death penalty does not deter murder. (I can imagine the joyful cries of those opposed to the death penalty who think they have caught me in a trap. That's right, I agree with you guys. Confused yet?). The purpose of any punishment is not to deter, but to enact justice and remove dangerous people from society. No punishment, not even capital punishment, can deter all crime. When people are desperate, they will not think of long-term consequences. This does not mean that all punishments should be eliminated because they cannot deter. Punishment has another purpose. Likewise, the death penalty cannot be eliminated because it cannot deter. This was never its purpose.

Death Penalty Should Be Fixed, Not Tossed

However, I still hold many reservations about the implementation of the death penalty in this country. To clarify, when I refer to implementation I am not referring to particular methods of execution. (After all, I believe that the electric chair and other "inhumane" methods of execution are only fitting for a convicted murderer). By implementation, I mean who gets executed. There is great disparity in the American judicial system regarding who gets executed. I would like to see a system where all murderers, regardless of their income level, have to pay for their crimes. I also fear that the innocent may be executed far too often in this country. To fix these problems, I propose that the government more aggressively encourage competent, experienced attorneys to give back to the community by becoming prosecutors. I also propose that standards in the investigatory process be tightened and better enforced to prevent innocent citizens from being accused of murder. With such new policies, many of the problems with the current judicial system could be fixed.

FAST FACT

In 2008, in the case *Baze v. Rees*, the Supreme Court ruled that lethal injection does not constitute cruel and unusual punishment and therefore does not violate the Eighth Amendment.

Philosophically, there is no good argument against capital punishment. It is morally justifiable. The only reservations are based on implementation and practicality. If both sides in the debate understood these facts, then solutions that could bring about the successful implementation of a death penalty could be found.

EVALUATING THE AUTHORS' ARGUMENTS:

Tyler Trumbach claims that the death penalty does not violate human rights because murderers are only denied their right to life after they are afforded due process and receive their legal rights, such as being given a fair trial. How do you think the other authors in this book would respond to the claim that murderers are afforded due process? Write one or two sentences for each author, and then state your own opinion.

Chapter 3

Is the Death Penalty Applied Fairly?

AN UNITED STATES CO

Some people believe that the death penalty is not applied fairly throughout the United States.

The Death Penalty Is Racist

Glen Stassen

"The blacker you look the more likely you are to be executed."

In the following viewpoint Glen Stassen argues that the death penalty—indeed, the entire criminal justice system—is biased against blacks. He offers statistics that show that people who kill white people are more often given the death penalty than people who kill blacks—a trend that implies that taking a white life is a more severe crime than taking a black life. Furthermore, Stassen states that black criminals are more likely to be sentenced to death than white criminals, and more likely to be imprisoned, too. Because of these inequities, Stassen argues the death penalty is racist and says the country must abolish such an unfair system. He calls on religious Americans to reject a system that kills, to teach that killing is wrong, and to oppose the death penalty in their state.

Stassen is a professor of Christian ethics at Fuller Theological Seminary and the author of *Kingdom Ethics*.

AS YOU READ, CONSIDER THE FOLLOWING QUESTIONS:
1. What states make up the "deathbelt" states, according to the author?
2. Since 1976, how many whites does the author say have been executed for killing a black person, and how many blacks have been executed for killing a white person?
3. According to Stassen, what percentage of prison inmates are black?

A t this year's [2008] annual meeting of the Society of Christian Ethics and Society of Jewish Ethics, William Montross of the Southern Center for Human Rights received a long, sustained, and enthusiastic applause—longer than for any plenary address I can remember. This year we met in Atlanta, Georgia, where Montross is a public defender. He gave us a challenge for all spiritual progressives, and for my particular Christian tradition as well.

Montross observed that the "Deathbelt" states (Virginia, the Carolinas, Georgia, Florida, Alabama, Mississippi, Louisiana, and Texas) have executed 90% of the human beings who were legally put to death in the United States in the last twenty years—and these are the states where most lynchings took place. Indeed, "Many say that today's executions are nothing more than yesterday's lynchings."

White Lives Worth More Than Black Lives

In Georgia, you are 4.3 times more likely to be sentenced to death for killing a white person than for killing a black. Similarly in Oklahoma, Illinois, Florida, Mississippi, North Carolina, and Alabama. Since 1976, fifteen whites have been executed for killing a black person in the United States; 283 blacks for killing a white victim. A Stanford University study concluded that the blacker you look the more likely you are to be executed.

Montross testified: "I saw a trial of a black man in Alabama. The whole jury was white men over forty; the jury was chosen in the morning, with no challenges; everyone in the courtroom was white. The prosecution put on its case. The defense attorney made no defense, but just said to the jury, 'If you can show this man mercy, you are better men than I am.' He got death."

A System Biased Against Blacks

African Americans comprise 26% of Alabama's population, yet only one of the forty-two elected district attorneys is black, and not one of the judges on Alabama's appellate court is black. Of all the states that have the death penalty, 98% of all U.S. chief district attorneys are white, and only 1% are black.

The criminal justice system as a whole is grossly biased against blacks and against the poor. Young blacks have a higher chance of going to

The Value of Life

Most of the murderers sentenced to death have murdered a white person. This is one of the reasons opponents of the death penalty say the system is racist.

Defendant-Victim Racial Combinations by Number and Percentage

	White Victim	Black Victim	Latino/a Victim	Asian Victim	Native American Victim
White Defendant	614 (52.57%)	15 (1.28%)	13 (1.11%)	4 (.34%)	0 (0%)
Black	243 (20.80%)	132 (11.30%)	15 (1.28%)	10 (.86%)	0 (0%)
Latino/a	39 (3.34%)	3 (.26%)	37 (3.17%)	2 (.17%)	0 (0%)
Asian	2 (.17%)	0 (0%)	0 (0%)	5 (.43%)	0 (0%)
Native American	13 (1.11%)	0 (0%)	0 (0%)	0 (0%)	2 (.17%)
TOTAL:	911 (78.00%)	150 (12.84%)	65 (5.57%)	21 (1.8%)	2 (.17%)

Note: In addition, there were 19 defendants executed for the murders of multiple victims of different races. Of those, 11 defendants were white, 5 black and 3 Latino (1.63%)

Taken from: Death Row U.S.A., Criminal Justice Project of the NAACP Legal Defense and Educational Fund, Inc., Summer 2009, p. 10.

prison than to college. In 2002, approximately 791,600 African American men were in prison, and only 603,000 were in higher education. The U.S. makes up 5% of the world's population, but it has 25% of the world's prison population, 48% of those in prison are black. They come out of prison with poor prospects for jobs, or for education. One-third of all African American men in Alabama have lost their right to vote. With the death penalty, once a person is executed, there is no way to correct a wrong sentence. This is a gross violation of the human rights of persons created in the image of God.

The glaring injustice is not only the systemic racial bias, but also the bias against whoever cannot afford an expensive defense lawyer. Arguing for the death penalty in his book, *For Capital Punishment*, Walter Berns admits that no one with money has ever gotten the death penalty in U.S. history.

Gary Ridgway murdered at least forty-eight women in Seattle. Eric Rudolph detonated a bomb at the Olympics in Atlanta, murdering two and injuring a hundred. Terry Nichols helped Timothy McVeigh kill 168 people by blowing up the federal building in Oklahoma City. McVeigh was executed but neither Gary, Eric, nor Terry got the death

Though Oklahoma City bomber Timothy McVeigh received the death penalty, his coconspirator, Terry Nichols, did not. Some believe that Nichols was protected from the death penalty because he is white.

penalty. Why? They were of huge public interest, so they were represented by competent lawyers. . . .

A Changing Tide

Opposition to the death penalty is now growing. Illinois Governor George Ryan pointed out that the error rate in Illinois for convicting persons to death had reached over 50%, as thirteen people have been exonerated and twelve have been put to death. He commuted all the remaining 167 death sentences to life. More recently, New Jersey has now abolished the death penalty.

The U.S. Supreme Court suspended the death penalty because of extensive evidence of racism and class bias. But then in 1976, they gave the go-ahead again. Yet 100 persons who had been sentenced to death since then were exonerated by April 9, 2002, because they were found to be erroneously convicted. With DNA evidence proving large numbers of convictions false, people are increasingly aware that the death penalty is biased, unjust, and full of errors.

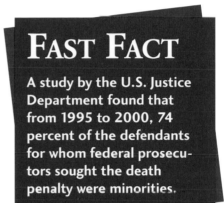

FAST FACT

A study by the U.S. Justice Department found that from 1995 to 2000, 74 percent of the defendants for whom federal prosecutors sought the death penalty were minorities.

The majority of Americans now say they prefer life without parole over the death penalty (*Los Angeles Times*, Dec. 15, 2006). It costs $12.3 million to execute someone, but $1 million to keep that person in jail for life. A life sentence allows an erroneous conviction to be corrected—as it was for that 100th exonerated person, Ray Krone, an innocent U.S. mailman who had been imprisoned for ten years, waiting for execution for a murder he had nothing to do with.

Support Waxes and Wanes

When Gallup [polling organization] has asked only the question, "Are you in favor of the death penalty for a person convicted of murder," without mentioning the alternative of life without parole, support for death increased while the United States was fighting World War II, eventually reaching 69% during the Korean War. But during the more peaceful times of the [Dwight D.] Eisenhower and [John F.] Kennedy administrations, support for the death penalty dropped dramatically to a minority of 42%. Then during the national frustration over the Vietnam War and the Watergate scandals of the [Richard M.] Nixon administration, combined with presidents who took a more self-righteous and punitive attitude, support grew steadily to 80% in 1994. Then it dropped to 63% during the [Bill] Clinton administration, but rose a bit to 69% during the [George] W. Bush years. Support seems to depend on whether the United States is at war, on economic frustration, and on the spirit of the presidential administration. If our next administration does not engage in new wars, and does not voice a self-righteous urge to punish, we can expect support to decline further. Already a majority prefer life without parole.

In 2006, executions dropped to a ten-year low, down to fifty-three (there had been ninety-eight in 1999). Texas killed most of those—twenty-four out of the fifty-three. But even in Texas, the number of death sentences handed down by courts dropped 65% in the ten years from 1996 to 2006. As the *Los Angeles Times* reported, "Public opinion seems to be changing."

We Will Win in Stages

We will win the victory over the death penalty in stages: If another state commutes or abolishes the death penalty, as Illinois and New Jersey did, this adds momentum. Thus one place to battle is in state legislatures and with state governors.

Many states are not giving out death penalties or are giving out far fewer ones. Thus another place to battle is in the court of public opinion, classrooms, churches and synagogues, and the media, all of which affect juries and prosecutors.

Data show the death penalty stimulates imitation, so states that kill criminals experience more homicides. But data also indicate there are effective ways to decrease homicides. We all need to learn and to teach what does work to prevent murders.

The related problem is class and race bias throughout the criminal justice system. Here the battle is for justice in sentencing generally, including drug sentencing, and adequate funding for the public defenders.

Churches in Georgia organized to visit the courts and the prisons, were shocked by what they saw, and persuaded the state finally to get a public defender system.

The Supreme Court is the eventual target. The new DNA evidence of many erroneous convictions, combined with the clear evidence of racism and class bias, combined with the shift in public opinion and in presidential leadership, can provide persuasive pressure. It may take some new appointees.

Montross is calling for churches and synagogues to visit the courts and prisons, and to mobilize our members to push for justice and human rights in the criminal justice system and against the death penalty. We are entering a time of hope for change. Will we answer?

EVALUATING THE AUTHORS' ARGUMENTS:

Glen Stassen bases his claim that the death penalty is racist on statistics showing that prisoners are more likely to get the death penalty for murdering whites than for murdering blacks. How do you think Kent Scheidegger, author of the following viewpoint, would respond to this claim? Be sure to quote from both texts in your answer.

Viewpoint 2

The Death Penalty Is Not Racist

Kent Scheidegger

"The defendants on death row are not there because of race."

The death penalty is not racially biased, argues Kent Scheidegger in the following viewpoint. Scheidegger points to studies that have found that the number of blacks sentenced to death is about the same as the number of blacks who commit crimes eligible for the death penalty. In other words, blacks are not being sentenced to death disproportionately or more often than any other racial group. He also argues that people who kill white and black victims are given the death penalty at the same rate when various factors are controlled for. Scheidegger says that the reforms put in place in the 1970s achieved their intended effect of eliminating discrimination and racism from the death penalty system. For these reasons he concludes that there is no reason to oppose the death penalty—in fact, he says communities would benefit from its increased use.

Scheidegger is the legal director of the Criminal Justice Legal Foundation, an organization that advocates for reduced rights for accused and convicted criminals.

Kent Scheidegger, "Maryland Study, When Properly Analyzed, Supports Death Penalty," Criminal Justice Legal Foundation, January 2003. Reproduced by permission.

AS YOU READ, CONSIDER THE FOLLOWING QUESTIONS:
  1. What concerns does Scheidegger say led the Supreme Court in 1972 to throw out then-existing death penalty laws?
  2. What did a study by Raymond Paternoster conclude about race and the death penalty, according to the author?
  3. What is the "race-of-victim effect," as described by Scheidegger, and what bearing does it have on his argument?

Opponents of capital punishment in Maryland are calling upon newly inaugurated Governor Robert Ehrlich to break his campaign promise and maintain the death penalty moratorium imposed by his predecessor. They cite a study released January 7 [2003] as a reason to do so. However, a closer look at the numbers points to the opposite conclusion. The study confirms that Maryland should not only lift the moratorium, but it should use the death penalty more often.

Studies Show No Racial Bias

The study was authorized by former Governor Parris Glendening. The lead author is University of Maryland Professor Raymond Paternoster, a well-known opponent of capital punishment. Its stated purpose is to examine "disparities" in capital sentencing by race or geography.

By far, the most powerful discrimination argument that could be made against capital punishment would be discrimination against minority defendants on the basis of their race. It was just such concerns that caused the Supreme Court to throw out all then-existing death penalty laws in 1972, resulting in a national overhaul of capital sentencing procedure. In Maryland, the study shows that the percentage of persons sentenced to death who are African-American is roughly the same as the percentage of persons who commit capital murder. After controlling for the legitimate differences in the cases, the study concludes "We have found no evidence that the race of the defendant matters in the processing of capital cases in the state."

This finding is particularly significant coming from a prominent opponent of capital punishment. It confirms similar results in studies

A prisoner in Texas learns that the U.S. Supreme Court has struck down the death penalty as discriminatory against minorities. The Court's decision triggered a national overhaul of capital sentencing by individual states.

in Georgia, California, New Jersey, and Nebraska, some of which were also conducted by death penalty opponents. The death penalty reforms put in place since the 1970s to eliminate discrimination are one of the great successes of modern criminal law. Widespread opposition to capital punishment among the African-American community is understandable if there is reason to believe it is imposed discriminatorily based on the race of the defendant, but these studies should put those fears to rest.

Other Racial Disparities Can Be Explained

The more difficult question is whether the death penalty is withheld in a discriminatory manner, i.e., whether murderers deserving of capital punishment are more likely to be let off with life when the victim is black.

Why Are So Many African Americans on Death Row?

As of July 1, 2009, African Americans made up over 41 percent of inmates on death row—yet African Americans make up only about 12 percent of the total U.S. population. Supporters of the death penalty say blacks are overrepresented on death row because they commit more crimes than other races. Opponents of the death penalty say the overrepresentation is due to a death penalty system that is racist and discriminatory.

Inmates on Death Row

Race	Number	Percentage
White	1,457	44.43
Black	1,364	41.60
Latino/Latina	379	11.56
Native American	37	1.13
Asian	41	1.25
Unknown	1	.03
Total:	3,279	

Taken from: *Death Row U.S.A.*, Criminal Justice Project of the NAACP Legal Defense and Educational Fund, Inc., Summer 2009, p. 1.

Using statewide total numbers, the Paternoster study found that a death sentence is statistically more likely when the victim is white. However, when the various counties of Maryland are examined, a different picture emerges. The so-called race-of-victim effect nearly disappears when the county of prosecution is considered. "When the prosecuting jurisdiction is added to the model, the effect for the victim's race diminishes substantially, and is no longer statistically significant," the study's summary says. Prosecutors in Baltimore City, the jurisdiction with the highest percentage of African-American population, were the least likely to seek the death penalty in eligible cases.

The study calls the variation by county "geographic disparity." I call it local government. The people in politically more conservative areas elect more tough-on-crime prosecutors. Those prosecutors seek the death penalty in a larger percentage of the cases for which it is allowed. Those areas also tend to have relatively larger percentages of white residents and hence a larger percentage of white homicide victims. Conversely, prosecutors elected in politically more liberal areas tend to seek the death penalty less often, and these areas tend to have large proportions of minority residents and minority victims of crime. The statistics that show up as a "race-of-victim effect" are not the result of racism in prosecution decisions but rather of the tough or soft prosecution policies chosen democratically by the people of each county when they elect their state's attorney.

Death Penalty Not Invoked Enough

If the numbers are correct, they indicate that the death penalty is not being invoked often enough in the predominately African-American areas of Maryland, to the detriment of crime victims in those areas. Several recent studies have confirmed what common sense has always told us—a death penalty that is actually enforced is a deterrent and saves innocent lives. For much too long, America's civil rights leadership has reflexively sided with the defense in matters of criminal law. The tragic result is a loss of advocacy for minority crime victims.

Properly interpreted, this study provides powerful support for Governor Ehrlich's promise to lift the moratorium. The absence of any discernible race-of-defendant effect means that the defendants on death row are not there because of race. The insufficient numbers of death sentences in black-victim cases means that defendants who deserved the death penalty may have escaped it because of race, but the constitutional protection against double jeopardy precludes any correction of those injustices. The best we can do is strive to protect all victims equally in the future.

EVALUATING THE AUTHORS' ARGUMENTS:

In this viewpoint Kent Scheidegger argues that the death penalty is not racist. In the previous viewpoint Glen Stassen argues that it is. After reading both viewpoints, with which author do you ultimately agree? Why? List at least three pieces of evidence that helped you form your opinion.

Innocent People Are Likely to Be Convicted and Executed

Ray Samuels

"Despite the best intentions . . . , innocent people have been convicted and sentenced to death."

The death penalty is prone to error, argues Ray Samuels in the following viewpoint. As a former chief of police, Samuels explains that he has witnessed brutal crimes that appear to be deserving of the death penalty. But he also knows from experience that the death penalty is an imperfect system in which there is a real and likely chance that an innocent person could be put to death. He explains that most death penalty–eligible convictions rest on human testimonies— but human testimony is often wrong, says Samuels. People mistakenly identify others and falsely remember details when witnessing a crime. Furthermore, many false confessions are obtained from accused criminals by overbearing and leading police. Samuels says the risk of putting an innocent to death is high and real—for all of these reasons he thinks the death penalty

Ray Samuels, "Capital Punishment Is a Costly Mistake," *Contra Costa Times*, December 20, 2008. Reproduced by permission of the author.

should be abolished and replaced with permanent imprisonment and community service programs that reduce crime before it occurs.

Samuels served as the chief of police in Newark, California, from 2003 to 2008.

AS YOU READ, CONSIDER THE FOLLOWING QUESTIONS:

1. What, according to the author, is the number one leading cause of wrongful convictions?
2. What is the number two leading cause of wrongful convictions, as cited by Samuels?
3. How much does the author say California could save per year if the death penalty were replaced with permanent imprisonment?

There are three words you rarely hear from law enforcement: We were wrong. We do not like to admit it, but, despite our best efforts, we sometimes get it wrong. A lifetime in law enforcement has taught me that lesson and showed me that, when it comes to the death penalty, the risk of a mistake is just too great.

A Witness to Horrific Crimes

For 33 years, I have worked as a police officer in the state of California. I have seen some truly horrific and shocking crimes; crimes for which the death penalty was designed. One gruesome example that comes immediately to mind is the vicious stabbing death of an infant in a crib to stop the child from crying during a triple murder and robbery.

In part because of crimes like this, I used to support the death penalty, but my experience in law enforcement has showed me that California would be better off if we replaced the death penalty with permanent imprisonment.

The Risk of Error Is Too Great

I believe that murderers need to be held accountable. Permanent imprisonment can accomplish this; it is a severe sentence and an appropriate punishment for individuals who commit the most heinous

Prisoners await execution on California's death row in San Quentin Prison, pictured here. Currently thirty-six hundred inmates have been sentenced to life without parole in lieu of the death penalty.

crimes. More than 3,600 men and women have been given this sentence in California. They will all die in prison.

Unlike the death penalty, this sentence allows for the correction of mistakes. Despite the best intentions of law enforcement, prosecutors, defense attorneys, judges and jurors, innocent people have been convicted and sentenced to death.

The margin for error with the death penalty is too great. Once imposed, it is a bell that cannot be unrung.

Humans Are Susceptible to Mistakes

As Chief of Police of Newark, I have done everything in my power to prevent wrongful convictions by implementing the best practices in my office. But like all police agencies, we are an organization of human beings, and like all things human, we are susceptible to mistakes. Even with the implementation of all the necessary precautions and strict supervisory and management oversight, the potential for error remains.

This year [2008], several pieces of legislation intended to prevent wrongful convictions, proposed by the California Commission on the Fair Administration of Justice, failed to advance out of the Senate Appropriations Committee because they cost too much to implement. These bills were not perfect by any means, but they were an attempt to prevent mistaken eyewitness identification, the number one cause of wrongful convictions, and false confessions, the second leading cause. The fact that we don't have the money to implement reforms such as these should concern us all.

Unfortunately, the situation is only going to get worse.

A Costly Mistake

Local jurisdictions are likely to lose a significant amount of state funding this year because of the severe financial crisis. This funding helps cities and counties provide essential services in the areas of public safety, emergency services, and health and children's services. Without it, our communities will no doubt suffer dire consequences.

At the same time, we continue to waste hundreds of millions on the state's dysfunctional death penalty. If we replaced the death penalty with a sentence of permanent imprisonment, the state would save more than $125 million each year. We haven't had an execution in California for three years. Are we any less safe as a result? I don't think so.

FAST FACT

The Death Penalty Information Center reports that since 1973, 138 people have been exonerated and freed from death row.

It is shocking to think that we are continuing to retain a costly and ineffective death penalty while refusing to fund measures that would prevent wrongful convictions and provide essential community services. If the millions of dollars currently spent on the death penalty were spent on investigating unsolved homicides, modernizing crime

Americans Think Innocent People Have Probably Been Executed

Nationwide polls show the overwhelming majority of Americans believe that innocent people are sometimes convicted of murder and have probably been executed for a crime they did not commit.

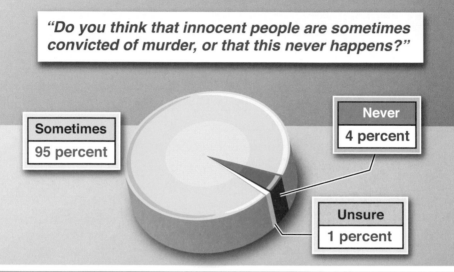

"Do you think that innocent people are sometimes convicted of murder, or that this never happens?"

Sometimes
95 percent

Never
4 percent

Unsure
1 percent

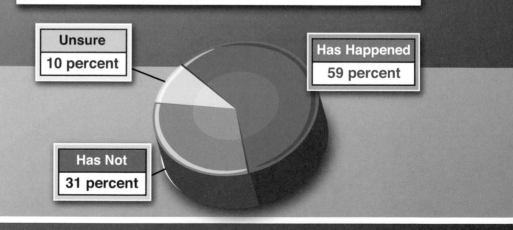

"Do you think a person has been executed under the death penalty who was, in fact, innocent of the crime he or she was charged with? Do you think this has happened in the past five years, or not?"

Unsure
10 percent

Has Happened
59 percent

Has Not
31 percent

Taken from: *Death Row U.S.A.*, Criminal Justice Project of the NAACP Legal Defense and Education Fund, Inc., Summer 2009, p. 10.

labs and expanding effective violence prevention programs, our communities would be much safer.

Holding onto the death penalty any longer would be a very costly mistake. Let's cut our losses and move on.

EVALUATING THE AUTHOR'S ARGUMENTS:

Ray Samuels is critical of law enforcement agencies, saying they have been wrong to pursue the death penalty and have made mistakes that could cause innocent people to be executed. As a former law enforcement official himself, does it surprise you that he would be critical of members of his own profession? Why or why not?

Viewpoint
4

Innocent People Are Not Likely to Be Convicted and Executed

Dudley Sharp

"*Of all the government programs in the world that put innocents at risk, is there one with a safer record and with greater protections than the US death penalty? Unlikely.*"

In the following viewpoint Dudley Sharp argues that innocent people are not likely to receive the death penalty. Sharp points out that the death penalty receives more oversight than any other government program. Because execution is such a serious and permanent punishment, capital cases receive intense scrutiny and are reviewed multiple times. Sharp says this process significantly reduces the chance for error. It is far more likely, in his opinion, for an innocent person to be sentenced to life in prison because those cases do not receive the same level of attention as death penalty cases. Sharp concludes that the only innocent people who are likely to be harmed by the death penalty are the people who will be killed by murderers who escape it.

Sharp is a leading supporter of and expert on the death penalty. He is resource director at Justice For All, a criminal justice reform group that advocates for the rights of violent crime victims.

AS YOU READ, CONSIDER THE FOLLOWING QUESTIONS:
1. According to Sharp, how many studies have found that the death penalty deters people from committing crime?
2. What percentage of murderers does the author say ask to receive, or plea bargain for, a death sentence?
3. What percentage of those sentenced to death since 1973 does Sharp say have been innocent?

O ften, the death penalty dialogue gravitates to the subject of innocents at risk of execution. Seldom is a more common problem reviewed. That is, how innocents are more at risk without the death penalty.

Of all the government programs in the world that put innocents at risk is there one with a safer record and with greater protections than the US death penalty?

Unlikely.

Extensive Due Process Lowers Risk

No knowledgeable and honest party questions that the death penalty has the most extensive due process protections in US criminal law.

Therefore, actual innocents are more likely to be sentenced to life imprisonment and more likely to die in prison serving under that sentence, than it is that an actual innocent will be executed. . . .

To state the blatantly clear, living murderers, in prison, after release or escape, are much more likely to harm and murder, again, than are executed murderers.

Although an obvious truism, it is surprising how often folks overlook the enhanced incapacitation benefits of the death penalty over incarceration.

Death Penalty Is Needed to Prevent Crime

Sixteen recent studies, inclusive of their defenses, find for death penalty deterrence.

Executions per Year

Since the death penalty was reinstated in 1976, fewer than 1,200 people have been executed. Death penalty cases account for a very small percentage of cases and typically take years to go through the courts. Supporters of the death penalty say this exhaustive process makes it very unlikely that an innocent person will be executed.

Number of executions since the 1976 reinstatement of capital punishment:

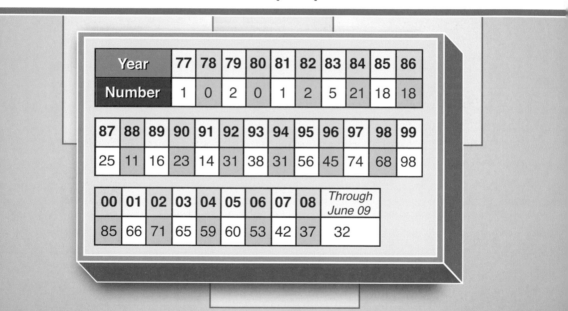

Year	77	78	79	80	81	82	83	84	85	86
Number	1	0	2	0	1	2	5	21	18	18

87	88	89	90	91	92	93	94	95	96	97	98	99
25	11	16	23	14	31	38	31	56	45	74	68	98

00	01	02	03	04	05	06	07	08	Through June 09
85	66	71	65	59	60	53	42	37	32

Taken from: *Death Row U.S.A.*, Criminal Justice Project of the NAACP Legal Defense and Education Fund, Inc., Summer 2009, p. 10.

A surprise? No.

Life is preferred over death. Death is feared more than life.

Some believe that all studies with contrary findings negate those 16 studies. They don't. Studies which don't find for deterrence don't say no one is deterred, but that they couldn't measure those deterred.

What prospect of a negative outcome/consequence doesn't deter some? There isn't one. Of course the death penalty deters. The only remaining dispute, never to be settled, is "how much does it deter?"

Not Even Murderers Want to Die

Some death penalty opponents argue against death penalty deterrence, stating that it's a harsher penalty to be locked up without any possibility of getting out.

Reality paints a very different picture.

What percentage of capital murderers seek a plea bargain to a death sentence? Zero or close to it. They prefer long term imprisonment.

What percentage of convicted capital murderers argue for execution in the penalty phase of their capital trial? Zero or close to it. They prefer long term imprisonment.

What percentage of death row inmates waive their appeals and speed up the execution process? Nearly zero. They prefer long term imprisonment.

This is not, even remotely, in dispute.

What of that more rational group, the potential murderers who choose not to murder, is it likely that they, like most of us, fear death more than life?

Life is preferred over death. Death is feared more than life.

Why Life in Prison Is Not Sufficient

Part of the anti–death penalty deception is that a life sentence, with no possibility of release, is a superior alternative to the death penalty. It's a lie. History tells us that lifers have many ways to get out: Pardon, commutation, escape, clerical error, change in the law, etc. There are few absolutes with sentencing. But,

> **FAST FACT**
>
> DNA was first used to exonerate a death row inmate in 1989. Supporters of the death penalty argue that the ability to use DNA testing to conclusively determine a person's guilt makes it unlikely that innocent people will be put to death.

here are two: the legislature can lessen the sentences of current inmates, retroactively, and the executive branch can lessen any individual sentence, at any time. This has been, actively, pursued, for a number of years, in many states, because of the high cost of life sentences and/or geriatric care, found to be $60,000–$90,000 per year per inmate.

Madison Hobley, who spent sixteen years on death row, talks to University of DePaul students about the judicial review process that led to his pardon for murder and arson convictions.

Innocent People Have Not Been Executed

Furthermore, possibly we have sentenced 25 actually innocent people to death since 1973, or 0.3% of those so sentenced. Those have all been released upon post conviction review. The anti–death penalty claims, that the numbers are significantly higher, are a fraud, easily discoverable by fact checking.

The innocents deception of death penalty opponents has been getting exposure for many years. Even the behemoth of anti–death penalty newspapers, *The New York Times*, has recognized that deception.

"To be sure, 30 or 40 categorically innocent people have been released from death row . . ." This when death penalty opponents were claiming the release of 119 "innocents" from death row. Death penalty opponents never required actual innocence in order for cases to be added to their "exonerated" or "innocents" list. They simply invented their own definitions for exonerated and innocent and deceptively shoe horned large numbers of inmates into those definitions—something easily discovered with fact checking.

There is no proof of an innocent executed in the US, at least since 1900.

The Death Penalty: 99.8 Percent Accurate

If we accept that the best predictor of future performance is past performance, we can, reasonably, conclude that the DNA cases will be excluded prior to trial, and that for the next 8000 death sentences, that we will experience a 99.8% accuracy rate in actual guilt convictions. This improved accuracy rate does not include the many additional safeguards that have been added to the system, over and above DNA testing.

In choosing to end the death penalty, or in choosing not to implement it, some have chosen to spare murderers at the cost of sacrificing more innocent lives.

> **EVALUATING THE AUTHOR'S ARGUMENTS:**
>
> Dudley Sharp argues that strict oversight, DNA testing, and other safeguards give the death penalty an accuracy rate of at least 99.8 percent or higher. In your opinion, is this an acceptable rate? Do you think the death penalty is worth having even if there is a chance of executing someone innocent, or do you think nothing less than 100 percent accuracy should be tolerated? Explain your reasoning.

Murderers Deserve to Be Treated As Human Beings

Terrica Redfield

Terrica Redfield is an attorney who represents criminals who have been sentenced to death. In the following viewpoint, she explains why she has chosen to represent murderers, saying they deserve to be treated like the human beings they are. In her opinion, the capital punishment system is flawed, biased, and an inappropriate punishment for those who have committed even the worst crimes. Redfield believes her clients are more than just the crimes they have committed—they are whole people with personalities, interests, and pain. Redfield says that representing murderers does not diminish the compassion she feels for their victims. Rather, it makes her realize that no one should be murdered—those who have been killed by murderers did not deserve to die, nor do the murderers deserve to be killed by the state. She rejects the characterization of murderers as monsters and urges Americans

> *"Death sentenced inmates and capital murder defendants are human beings. They are not monsters, or animals."*

Terrica Redfield, "Human Side of Death Penalty Defense," *Atlanta Lawyer*, November 2008, pp. 10–11. Reproduced by permission.

to remember that even criminals are human beings who do not deserve execution.

Redfield works for the Southern Center for Human Rights, a group that addresses human rights, improper incarceration, and capital punishment.

AS YOU READ, CONSIDER THE FOLLOWING QUESTIONS:
1. List at least five "inherent problems" Redfield says have currently befallen America's capital punishment system.
2. Describe the author's experience at the Cook County Jail and how it changed her life.
3. According to Redfield, what do her clients—murderers—have in common with everyone else?

"Doesn't she realize that he's a monster?" That was the question that one of the officers at Holman Prison in Atmore, Alabama struggled with each time he observed me visiting with my death-sentenced clients. As he saw me walking to my car at the conclusion of my visit, he took the opportunity to ask me about it.

An Opportunity for Conversation
As it usually is when I visit my clients on death row in Alabama, it had been a long day. I was on the road at 6:00 a.m., driving four hours from Atlanta to Atmore. I had visited with my clients for five hours, and I was headed to my car getting ready to make the long trip back to Atlanta when I was approached by an officer who asked if he could ask me a question. He was driving around in a pick-up owned, I assumed, by the prison. As I placed my notepad and pen in the trunk and retrieved my purse, he pulled the truck up a few feet away from my car. He never got out of the truck, and he never turned off the motor.

"Do you believe in the death penalty?" he asked. "No," I replied. Then he asked the logical follow-up question, "Why not?" For years, I have been visiting clients charged with capital murder or sentenced to death, and no prison or jail officer had ever asked me about my opinions on the death penalty, up until that point. I have been questioned about my age, how long I have been practicing, and even my relationship status on numerous occasions. I had never been asked how I could represent the clients that I choose to represent. I thought to myself, "I don't have time to get into this. I need to get on the road." I quickly rattled off something about my religious beliefs, hoping that would be enough to satisfy him. It was not.

He explained that he had been thinking about the death penalty. He had asked the warden and others about their opinions about the death penalty, in an attempt to reconcile his own beliefs. He said he supported the death penalty, and he was hoping that I could provide the silver bullet that would change his mind. I suddenly felt unprepared. I did not have a silver bullet. I purposely do not get into arguments with people who adamantly support the death penalty. I simply listen to their opinions, provide the facts, tell the stories, and expect that they will consider those facts as they struggle with the issue. I never imagined that I would be expected to say one thing, or a series of things, that could immediately convince a person who supports the death penalty that they no longer should. Even in litigating my cases, I do not attempt to convince fact-finders that the death penalty should be abolished; rather I try to convince them that the death penalty is inappropriate for my particular client. I was under pressure. How could I convince this guy that the death penalty is wrong in the time I had standing outside my car at the prison? I decided that it could not be done, and I told him so.

"Doesn't She Know That He's a Monster?"
He explained that he sometimes observed me visiting with my clients, talking and sometimes laughing with them, and he often thought to himself, "Doesn't she know that he's a monster?" Wow. A monster? I was shocked by the sheer honesty of the statement. "No, sir," I told him, "I don't think my clients are monsters." He, although being an officer at the prison, apparently was like most people: he only knew my clients by the crimes for which they had been convicted. If I had been thinking, I would have spent some time exploring that fact. Instead, I rambled on about each person having their own journey that leads them to the answer to that question. I explained that there was no way that I could, in the limited time that both of us had, tell him everything he needed to know about what is wrong with the death

penalty in order for him to make a more informed decision about his support for the death penalty. I thanked him for at least struggling with the issue and asking these important questions, and I expressed my wish that I had more time to talk with him about it. I then got in my car and headed home.

I felt like dirt the entire ride home. I kept thinking that I had let my clients down. I had let myself down. I had the opportunity to convince one more person that the death penalty, at least as currently administered, is wrong, and I failed. It was a really long drive back home that day.

Murderers Are Still Human Beings

If I had it to do over again, I probably would not even attempt to answer the question right then and there. I would suggest that we make an appointment to discuss the issue further over coffee or at his church or some other place where he could ask me all the questions that were on his mind and we could really talk about the issue without me

A South Carolina death row inmate stands in his cell, where he is confined for twenty-three hours of every day.

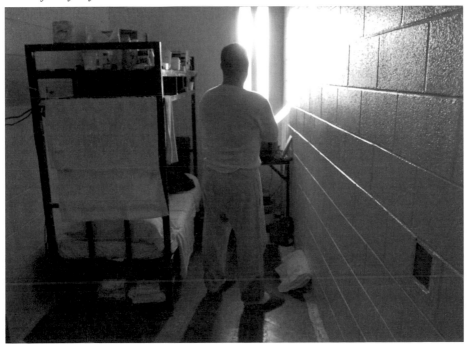

feeling forced to give my answer in sound bites or clichés. I hopefully would detail in a clear manner some of the inherent problems with our current system of capital punishment, such as its disproportionate effect on racial minorities and the poor, the woeful lack of adequate funding for capital defense attorneys, the shocking number of persons who have been wrongfully convicted of capital crimes, the lack of adequate training for some capital defense attorneys, the emotional toll a death penalty trial takes on all parties involved, the enormous financial costs to taxpayers who could better use the money to pay for more school buses, fire fighters, and other needs of their communities, and so on.

But more than that, I would try to convey the following two things:

1) Death sentenced inmates and capital murder defendants are human beings.

They are not monsters, or animals, or any of the other non-human terms often used to describe them. I know that is hard to believe for those who have only read the horrifying details of some of the crimes committed. Sometimes, even I think to myself, "Oh my God, why?" or "How could someone do that?" On some occasions, I have been moved to tears at the nature of the crimes committed. That anger, disgust, and sadness are natural reactions to a very unnatural occurrence. It is the answers to the questions of "Why?" and "How?", however, that move people from that awful space to a place where mercy can be considered and where justice has a chance.

Because jurors and judges who are charged with the decision of whether someone should live or die for the crimes they committed need to know about the person whose life is in their hands and how he or she came to be at a place where others sit in judgment of the worthiness of their life, justice requires that I investi-

"Maybe this will teach you that it's morally wrong to kill people!"

gate my clients' entire lives, even generations before they were born, and compellingly present my clients' humanity. In trying to figure out the "hows" and the "whys," I come to know the complete human beings, not just the worst things they have ever done in their lives. That, more than anything else, is what motivates me to keep doing this work.

No One Deserves to Be Murdered

2) Representing death sentenced inmates does not blind me to the concerns of victims.

I believe in what I do, but I am not a robot, and I do not need to be a robot to be an effective advocate for my clients. I understand that no one deserves to be murdered, that the victims whose lives were taken prematurely deserved better, that their lives were important, and that they were loved. Those facts do not escape me, because I know that tragedy can happen to anyone, and no one ever deserves it.

I have been working in some capacity with death penalty defense for my entire legal career. I came to this work through a discovery process after my visit to the Cook County Jail as a college student forced me to evaluate for the first time my feelings about the criminal justice system. I recall being on a tour of the jail with law students who were interning at firms in Chicago that summer. When one of the law students asked the officer to stage a fight among the inmates for our entertainment, something went off inside of me. Growing up in rural Mississippi, where for years gun safety was taught in middle school, I was certainly not someone who had much sympathy for criminals. In fact, in considering law school, I just knew that I would never do criminal defense work, because I didn't want to work with "crazy" people. But that day, I was shocked and appalled. I thought to myself, "This is a jail, so some of these people haven't even been convicted of anything, and here are future leaders of our country who have such low sense of human decency that they would request a staged brawl for their own entertainment. What is our world coming to?"

Why I Represent Murderers

The other thing that struck me as I walked through the jail looking at the inmates like we were in a zoo was that the vast majority of the inmates we encountered looked like me—they were African-American. I thought, "Something's wrong with this picture."

As a law student I volunteered on a post-conviction case, and I was hooked. I started learning more about the death penalty, and the more I learned, the angrier I became about the injustice of the entire system. The one particular aspect of the death penalty that led me to this work was the inherent racism and classism of the entire process, but that is not what keeps me in the work.

I was attracted to death penalty defense because I was appalled at the racial disparities in the system. I continue to practice death penalty defense because I'm committed to my clients and I care. After visiting with one of the clients for whom he had conducted legal research on his case, one of our interns remarked, "That's not what I expected." The client was articulate, smart, well-versed in national and international affairs, and funny. "I know," I replied. "It's not what anyone expects." My clients hurt, laugh, cry, and love like the rest of us. I would not have known that from reading the newspaper articles about the crimes or watching the news reports on television. I found that out by getting to know them.

EVALUATING THE AUTHOR'S ARGUMENTS:

Terrica Redfield says her experiences as a death row attorney have helped her to see convicted murderers as people with complicated and important personalities, feelings, and thoughts. After reading about her experiences, do you agree with her? Did she convince you to see murderers less as monsters and more as human beings? Why or why not?

Murderers Deserve to Be Executed

William Murchison

"Not to inflict proportionate punishment [on a murderer] would be the same as saying, there, there, you've been a bad boy."

In the following viewpoint William Murchison argues there should be no sympathy for those who commit murder. He discusses how death penalty opponents have complained that inmates may feel pain during their executions and thus seek the abolition of the death penalty on these and other grounds. Murchison says it is inappropriate to go to lengths to ensure that murderers are made comfortable—they killed others and thus deserve the worst punishment society can offer. He thinks it is wrong to have sympathy for murderers or to allow them to live out their lives in any modicum of comfort. He concludes that executions are not meant to deter bad behavior but to forcefully state that some actions—and some people—are so wicked they cannot be tolerated. The death penalty is the only punishment that sends this message and thus Murchison says it should be retained.

Murchison is a nationally syndicated columnist and holds various editorial roles for the *Lone Star Report, Foundations, Human Life Review,* and *Chronicles.*

AS YOU READ, CONSIDER THE FOLLOWING QUESTIONS:
1. What crime does the author say was committed by Ralph Baze?
2. How do Adolf Hitler, Joseph Stalin, and Saddam Hussein factor into Murchison's argument?
3. Why does the author think it is ridiculous to allow a certain murderer from Kentucky to plead for exemption from suffering?

Such is the state of modern society that the U.S. Supreme Court gets the job of deciding how much pain the victim of capital punishment feels—never mind what kind of pain the victim's victims may have felt.

Kind of interesting—and very modern: part and parcel of the process by which our institutions attempt to work off guilt for all manner of things done in the past and now perceived as somehow brutal and unjust.

A court decision adverse to the state of Kentucky's procedure for executing convicted murderer—a drug "cocktail" that knocks out the victim before killing him—wouldn't exactly end capital punishment, or even capital punishment via drugs. What it would do is send state lawmakers re-legislating to identify and approve a pain-free knockout punch.

The Kentucky cocktail is standard 21st century operating procedure —a replacement for the electric chair, which in turn replaced the noose.

"This Is an Execution, Not Surgery"

A lawyer arguing for mercy on Ralph Baze—who executed a sheriff and deputy trying to serve a warrant on him—insisted the way to go is a single dose of barbiturates. Justice Antonin Scalia wanted to know why pain was such a central consideration in the legal equation. "This is an execution, not surgery," Scalia said.

Well, yes. And no. That it *is* an execution is what matters to growing numbers of Americans working to put capital punishment itself to death. The technique is, object to everything about the death penalty—fairness, pain, cost, international opinion, the prospect of executing the innocent. Death by a thousand cuts is the prescription for the death penalty.

Convicted murderer Ralph S. Baze brought suit against the state of Kentucky to challenge its use of a "lethal cocktail" for his pending execution and arguing for the use of barbiturates instead.

Any time you have to put the matter to lawmakers—as would be the case if the Supreme Court were to disallow the Kentucky cocktail—is a chance for a debate on the whole premise that the state may take a murderer's life. You're debating means, say, and someone says no, let's talk about ends and about the supposed moral horror of an execution.

The Backlash Against Capital Punishment

Only last month [in December 2007], liberal New Jersey became the first state in 42 years to abolish the death penalty, which it wasn't using anyway. Polls show public support for capital punishment at 62 percent

—though large, it's also shown to be the lowest in three decades. Capital punishment foes would doubtless peel off more of these adversaries once they got rolling. Considerable help would come from liberal Christians . . . with their worldly concerns for "social justice."

It fascinates—the gift of 21st century society for turning inside out its old norms without devoting undue attention to the question of whether those norms made the sense we once supposed they did.

What about capital punishment? Does it suddenly, after all these centuries, make *no* sense? The principle, I mean, not every application, as in the burnings-alive of the Reformation era—none of which we're likely to imitate as a society.

It Is Appropriate to Execute Monsters

Would it have made sense to spare the lives of [Nazi leaders Hermann] Goering and [Heinrich] Himmler rather than visit on them personally and publicly the consequences of their war crimes? What of [Nazi leader Adolf] Hitler himself, had he survived the war? What of [Soviet dictator Joseph] Stalin, could he have been caught by the representatives of a decent Russian regime? What of [Iraqi dictator] Saddam Hussein, who was indeed caught and hanged?

Extreme examples? I raise them for purposes of affirming the underlying purpose of capital punishment, which really isn't that of deterring bad behavior; it's that of making a declaration about a particular human act, one so wicked that not to inflict proportionate punishment would be the same as saying, there, there, you've been a bad boy, but that won't stop us from caring for you and feeding and housing you and making sure your plasma TV works right.

No Sympathy for Murderers

Baze, our Kentucky murderer, pleads for exemption from suffering. Why, all he did was kill two men in cold blood. What do we learn

Americans Think the Death Penalty Is Applied Fairly

Annual polls show that a majority of Americans consistently think the death penalty is a just punishment that is applied fairly, without bias or error.

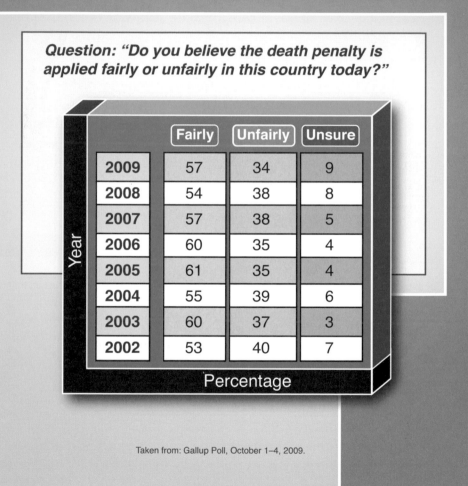

Question: "Do you believe the death penalty is applied fairly or unfairly in this country today?"

Year	Fairly	Unfairly	Unsure
2009	57	34	9
2008	54	38	8
2007	57	38	5
2006	60	35	4
2005	61	35	4
2004	55	39	6
2003	60	37	3
2002	53	40	7

Percentage

Taken from: Gallup Poll, October 1–4, 2009.

from avenging them? the soft-hearted inquire. We learn their human worth, for starters—their unique place in the created order, as disdained by the man who shot them. We learn of their families' pain and suffering. Lastly, we learn of classic justice—"to each his own"— and the urgency of restoring it to a central place in modern affairs.

The renewed, re-quickened attack on the agonies of capital punishment may have its success stories to relate. Whether these stories will speak with equal conviction as to the agonies involved in maintaining the moral order—we wait to see.

> **EVALUATING THE AUTHORS' ARGUMENTS:**
>
> William Murchison and the other pro-death-penalty authors represented in this anthology all believe that the death penalty is a just and appropriate punishment for people who have committed murder. Based on the texts you have read, write a five paragraph essay on whether or not you ultimately agree. Include at least three distinct reasons in your answer.

Facts About the Death Penalty

Editor's note: These facts can be used in reports to add credibility when making important points or claims.

Facts About Executions

According to the Bureau of Justice Statistics:

- As of early 2009, thirty-five states and the federal government employed the death penalty.
- In 2005 there were sixty executions.
- In 2006 there were fifty-three executions.
- In 2007 there were forty-two executions.
- In 2008 there were thirty-seven executions.
- In 2009 there were fifteen executions.
- States and jurisdictions that employ the death penalty are: Alabama, Arizona, Arkansas, California, Colorado, Connecticut, Delaware, Florida, Georgia, Idaho, Indiana, Illinois, Kansas, Kentucky, Louisiana, Maryland, Mississippi, Missouri, Montana, Nebraska, Nevada, New Hampshire, North Carolina, Ohio, Oklahoma, Oregon, Pennsylvania, South Carolina, South Dakota, Tennessee, Texas, Utah, Virginia, Washington, Wyoming, the U.S. government and the U.S. military.
- States and jurisdictions that do not employ the death penalty are: Alaska, Hawaii, Iowa, Maine, Massachusetts, Michigan, Minnesota, New Jersey, New Mexico, New York, North Dakota, Rhode Island, Vermont, West Virginia, Wisconsin, and the District of Columbia.
- Kansas, New Hampshire, and the U.S. military are the only jurisdictions that have death penalty laws but have not conducted any executions since 1976.
- The top executing states in 2008 were:
  - Texas (eighteen executions)
  - Virginia (four executions)
  - Georgia and South Carolina (three executions each)
  - As of 2010, five execution methods were legal in the United States; the most common method was lethal injection.

- Idaho, Oklahoma, and Utah allow execution by firing squad.
- Delaware, New Hampshire, and Washington allow execution by hanging.
- Arizona, California, Missouri, and Wyoming allow execution by lethal gas.
- Alabama, Arkansas, Florida, Illinois, Kentucky, Oklahoma, South Carolina, Tennessee, and Virginia allow execution by electrocution.
- Of the thirty-seven people who were executed in 2008:
  - twenty were white.
  - seventeen were black.
  - thirty-seven were male.
  - thirty-six executions were by lethal injection.
  - one was by electrocution.

According to the Death Penalty Information Center:
- Death penalty costs can average $10 million more per year per state than life sentences.
- California spends more than $130 million a year on its capital punishment system and has not executed anyone in four years.
- A new death row would cost California $400 million to construct.
- Florida spends an average of $24 million per execution.

Facts About Death Row

According to the Bureau of Justice Statistics:
- In 2005 there were 3,254 inmates on death row.
- In 2006 there were 3,228 inmates on death row.
- In 2007 there were 3,215 inmates on death row.
- In 2008 there were 3,207 inmates on death row.
- As of 2008:
  - California had the most inmates on death row: 669.
  - Florida had the second most inmates on death row: 390.
  - Texas had the third most inmates on death row: 354.
  - Wyoming and New Hampshire had the fewest number of inmates on death row: 1 in each state.
- Of 3,207 people on death row in 2008:
  - 98.2 percent were male.
  - 1.8 percent were female.
  - 56.1 percent were white.
  - 41.7 percent were black.

- 2.2 percent were another race.
- 13.5 percent had an eighth grade education or less.
- 36.5 percent had a ninth to eleventh grade education.
- 40.8 percent were high school graduates or the equivalent.
- 9.2 percent had some college.
- 22.2 percent were married.
- 20.1 percent were divorced/separated.
- 2.9 percent were widowed.
- 54.7 percent had never married.
- Between 1977 and 2008, 7,658 people have been under sentence of death.
  - Of these, 15 percent have been executed.
  - 5 percent have died from causes other than execution.
  - 38 percent received other sentences.
  - In 2008, 111 new inmates were admitted to death row, the smallest number of admissions since 1973.
- In 2008, 119 inmates were removed from death row.
  - 37 were executed.
  - 82 were removed by other methods, including overturned sentences or convictions, commutations of sentence, and deaths by means other than execution.

The Death Penalty Information Center reports that since 1973, 138 people have been exonerated and freed from death row.

American Opinions of the Death Penalty
According to a 2009 Gallup poll:
- 65 percent of Americans favor the death penalty.
- 31 percent oppose it.
- 5 percent are unsure.*
- 20 percent think the death penalty is imposed too often.
- 24 percent think it is imposed the right amount of time.
- 49 percent think the death penalty is not imposed often enough.
- 7 percent are unsure.
- 57 percent think the death penalty is applied fairly.
- 34 percent think the death penalty is not applied fairly.
- 9 percent are unsure.
- 59 percent think an innocent person has probably been executed within the last five years.

- 31 percent do not think an innocent person has been executed within the last five years.
- 10 percent are unsure.
- 62 percent of Americans describe the death penalty as "morally acceptable."
- 30 percent of Americans describe the death penalty as "morally wrong."

A 2009 CNN poll found the following about the death penalty:
- 53 percent of Americans think the death penalty is a better punishment for murder than life in prison without parole.
- 46 percent think life in prison without parole is a better punishment for murder than the death penalty.
- 2 percent are unsure.*
- 26 percent of Americans regard the death penalty as cruel and unusual punishment.
- 73 percent do not regard the death penalty as cruel and unusual punishment.
- 1 percent are unsure.

According to a 2008 Harris poll:
- 42 percent of Americans think the death penalty deters crime.
- 52 percent think it probably does not have much effect on crime.
- 6 percent are unsure.

According to a 2009 *USA Today*/Gallup poll:
- 77 percent think convicted terrorists should get the death penalty.
- 18 percent think convicted terrorists should not get the death penalty.
- 5 percent are unsure.

Figures add up to greater than 100 percent due to rounding.

Organizations to Contact

The editors have compiled the following list of organizations concerned with the issues debated in this book. The descriptions are derived from materials provided by the organizations. All have publications or information available for interested readers. The list was compiled on the date of publication of the present volume; the information provided here may change. Be aware that many organizations take several weeks or longer to respond to inquiries, so allow as much time as possible for the receipt of requested materials.

Amnesty International USA
5 Penn Plaza
New York, NY 10001
(212) 807-8400
Web site: www.amnesty-usa.org

Amnesty International is a global organization that works toward fair and prompt trials for political prisoners and an end to torture and executions. It opposes the death penalty for several reasons, including the belief that it constitutes cruel and unusual punishment.

Citizens United for Alternatives to the Death Penalty (CUADP)
PMB 335
2603 Dr. Martin Luther King Jr. Hwy.
Gainesville, FL 32609
(800) 973-6548
e-mail: cuadp@cuadp.org
Web site: www.cuadp.org

CUADP works to end the death penalty in the United States through campaigns of public education about viable death penalty alternatives and the promotion of tactical grassroots activism.

Death Penalty Information Center (DPIC)
1015 Eighteenth St. NW, #704

Washington, DC 20036
(202) 289-2275
Web site: www.deathpenaltyinfo.org

The DPIC believes capital punishment is discriminatory, costly, and likely results in the execution of innocent persons. It conducts research into public opinion on the death penalty. Its Web site contains numerous articles and other resources on the death penalty, including a searchable database of all persons who have been executed since 1976.

Journey of Hope
PO Box 210390
Anchorage, AK 99521-0390
Web site: www.journeyofhope.org

This organization is run by murder victims' family members, death row family members, family members of the executed, the exonerated, and others who oppose the death penalty and seek alternatives to capital punishment.

Justice Fellowship
44180 Riverside Pkwy.
Lansdowne, VA 20176
Web site: www.justicefellowship.org

Although this Christian organization takes no official position on the death penalty, it works to reform the justice system to reflect a concept of victim-offender reconciliation. Its Web site offers articles and updates on developments regarding death penalty issues.

Justice for All
PO Box 55159
Houston, TX 77255
(713) 935-9300
Web site: www.jfa.net

This pro-death-penalty organization focuses on victims' rights and offers a wealth of information on death-penalty-related issues. Its activities include circulating online petitions to keep violent offenders from being paroled early and publishing the monthly newsletter the *Voice of Justice.*

The Moratorium Campaign
586 Harding Blvd.
Baton Rouge, LA 70807
Web site: www.moratoriumcampaign.org

This anti-death-penalty organization was founded by Sister Helen Prejean, author of the book *Dead Man Walking.* In addition to seeking the abolition of the death penalty, the organization petitions doctors to refrain from participating in lethal injection executions.

Murder Victims' Families for Reconciliation
2100 M St. NW, Ste. 170-296
Washington, DC 20037
(877) 896-4702
Web site: www.mvfr.org

This national organization comprises family members of victims of both homicide and executions who oppose the death penalty in all cases. Compelling family stories are a key feature of the organization's Web site.

National Coalition to Abolish the Death Penalty (NCADP)
1705 DeSales St. NW, 5th Fl.
Washington, DC 20036
(202) 331-4090
e-mail: info@ncadp.org
Web site: www.ncadp.org

The NCADP is a collection of more than 115 groups that together work to outlaw the death penalty and stop executions in the United States. The organization compiles statistics on the death penalty and publishes numerous information packets, pamphlets, and other research materials.

Witness to Innocence
PO Box 34725

Philadelphia, PA 19101
(215) 471-7090
e-mail: info@witnesstoinnocence.org
Web site: www.witnesstoinnocence.org

Witness to Innocence is the nation's only organization composed of and formed by and for exonerated death row survivors and their loved ones. Members actively work to end the death penalty on the grounds that the criminal justice system is flawed and likely to incarcerate— and execute—innocent people. The group's Web site features compelling stories from formerly incarcerated people.

For Further Reading

Books

Allen, Howard W., and Jerome M. Clubb. *Race, Class, and the Death Penalty: Capital Punishment in American History.* Albany: State University of New York Press, 2009. The authors explore how frequently the death penalty has been used and the characteristics of the executed. Concludes that while the use of the death penalty has progressively declined, disparities in the use of capital punishment between social groups and regions have persisted into the twenty-first century.

Baumgartner, Frank R., Suzanna L. De Boef, and Amber E. Boydstun. *The Decline of the Death Penalty and the Discovery of Innocence.* New York: Cambridge University Press, 2008. Discusses how prosecutors, judges, and juries across the country have begun to give much greater credence to the possibility of mistakes in the application of the death penalty.

Bohm, Robert. *Ultimate Sanction: Understanding the Death Penalty Through Its Many Voices and Many Sides.* New York: Kaplan, 2010. Explores issues surrounding the death penalty through the voices of people who have been directly affected by its application.

Burkhead, Michael Dow. *A Life for a Life: The American Debate over the Death Penalty.* Jefferson, NC: McFarland, 2009. Explores the various trends in public opinion that influence crime prevention efforts, create public policy, and reform criminal law. Examines eight core issues surrounding the use of execution: cruel and unusual punishment, discrimination, deterrence, due process, culpability, scripture, innocence, and justice.

Garland, David. *Peculiar Institution: America's Death Penalty in an Age of Abolition.* Cambridge, MA: Belknap Press, 2010. Tells a fascinating story that illuminates why the death penalty is so problematic and yet so well suited to American practices.

Gerber, Rudolph J., and John M. Johnson. *The Top Ten Death Penalty Myths: The Politics of Crime Control.* Santa Barbara, CA: ABC-CLIO,

2007. Dismantles the arguments of death penalty supporters one by one, demonstrating why the death penalty is wrong and why capital punishment does not work.

Gleason, Ron. *The Death Penalty on Trial: Taking of a Life for a Life Taken.* Ventura, CA: Nordskog, 2009. Examines the controversy over the death penalty by examining history, law, and capital punishment's biblical mandate.

Lane, Charles. *Stay of Execution: Why the Death Penalty Has Declined and Why We Still Need It.* Lanham, MD: Rowman & Littlefield, 2010. Analyzes the decline in the use of the death penalty and its moral and political implications. Argues that capital punishment should be preserved and proposes major reforms to address its inequities and inconsistencies.

Lanier, Charles S., William J. Bowers, and James R. Acker. *The Future of America's Death Penalty: An Agenda for the Next Generation of Capital Punishment Research.* Durham, NC: Carolina Academic Press, 2008. Identifies the most critical issues confronting the future of capital punishment in the United States and the steps that must be taken to make informed policy judgments.

Lyon, Andrea. *Angel of Death Row: My Life as a Death Penalty Defense Lawyer.* New York: Kaplan, 2010. A death penalty defense lawyer recounts how she has successfully argued for the lives of her clients to be spared.

Paternoster, Raymond, Robert Brame, and Sarah Bacon. *The Death Penalty: America's Experience with Capital Punishment.* New York: Oxford University Press, 2007. Presents a balanced exploration of arguments for and against capital punishment. Coverage draws on legal, historical, philosophical, economic, sociological, and religious points of view.

Sundby, Scott E. *A Life and Death Decision: A Jury Weighs the Death Penalty.* New York: Palgrave Macmillan, 2007. Uses the personal stories of death penalty case jurors to offer an account of what occurs behind the jury room doors. Explores issues such as jury instructions, jury room setup and other procedures.

Periodicals and Internet Sources

America. "The Price of Death," October 26, 2009. www.americamag azine.org/content/article.cfm?article_id=11929&comments=1.

Amnesty International. "The Death Penalty v. Human Rights: Why Abolish the Death Penalty?" September 2007. www.amnesty.org/en/library/asset/ACT51/002/2007/en/3c7c3501-d36a-11dd-a329-2f46302a8cc6/act510022007en.pdf.

Berns, Walter. "Religion and the Death Penalty: Can We Have One Without the Other?" *Weekly Standard,* February 4, 2008. www.weeklystandard.com/Content/Public/Articles/000/000/014/656wdzwt.asp?pg=1.

Boteach, Shmuley. "The Death Penalty for Terrorists," *Jerusalem Post,* July 21, 2008. www.jpost.com/servlet/Satellite?cid=1215331047048&pagename=JPArticle%2FShowFull.

Bright, Stephen B. "The Death Penalty and the Society We Want," *Pierce Law Review,* vol. 6, no. 3, 2008. www.schr.org/files/steve_dp_society_want.pdf.

Campbell, Tom. "It's Time to Stop Executing People," *Greensboro (NC) News & Record,* April 17, 2009. www.news-record.com/content/2009/04/17/article/tom_campbell_it_s_time_to_stop_executing_people.

Death Penalty Information Center. *Smart on Crime: Reconsidering the Death Penalty in a Time of Economic Crisis.* Washington, DC: Death Penalty Information Center, October 2009. www.death penalty info.org/documents/CostsRptFinal.pdf.

Feehery, John. "Is the Death Penalty Defensible?" *The Hill,* September 1, 2009. http://thehill.com/blogs/pundits-blog/crime/56927-is-the-death-penalty-defensible.

Hall, Harold. "A Sentence Too Close to Death: Wrongly Convicted, I Am Proof That the State Should Reconsider Execution," *Los Angeles Times,* March 27, 2008. http://articles.latimes.com/2008/mar/27/opinion/oe-hal27.

Hastings, Deborah. "To Execute or Not: A Question of Cost?" *USA Today,* March 7, 2009. www.usatoday.com/news/nation/2009-03-07-exexpensive-to-execute_N.htm.

Herron, Aundré M. "The Death Penalty Is Not Civilized," *Sacramento (CA) Bee,* April 20, 2008.

Howard, Stanley. "No Humane Way to Kill," *Socialist Worker,* May 13, 2008. http://socialistworker.org/2008/05/13/no-humane-way-to-kill.

Jackson, Lester. "A Death Penalty Red Herring: The Inanity and Hypocrisy of Perfection," TCS Daily.com, October 2009. http://tcsdaily.com/printArticle.aspx? ID=102909A.

————. "The Subversion of Capital Punishment," TCS Daily.com, May 28, 2009. http://tcsdaily.com/article.aspx?id=052709A.

Kovarsky, Lee. "Opposing the Death Penalty Is Not About Innocence," *Salon*, September 11, 2009. http://mobile.salon.com/opinion/feature/2009/09/11/death_penalty/index.html.

Lain, Corinna Barrett. "The New Case Against the Death Penalty," *Christian Science Monitor*, May 11, 2009. www.csmonitor.com/2009/0511/p09s01-coop.html.

Lee, Jin Hee, Vincent Southerland, and Christina Swarns. "A Cause for Dissent: The Death Penalty's Cruel and Unusual Punishment," *Defenders Online*, September 29, 2009. www.thedefendersonline.com/2009/09/29/a-cause-for-dissent-the-death-penalty%E2%80%99s-cruel-and-unusual-punishment/.

Lindsay, Lance. "We Can't Afford the Death Penalty," New America Media.com, March 4, 2009. http://news.ncmonline.com/news/view_article.html?article_id=0b51d00d8e7f9c65f192139df5ffd315.

Lowe, Wesley. "Capital Punishment vs. Life Without Parole," WesleyLowe.com, July 22, 2009. www.wesleylowe.com/cp.html#life.

Muhlhausen, David B. "The Death Penalty Deters Crime and Saves Lives," testimony before the Senate Subcommittee on the Constitution, Civil Rights, and Property Rights, Committee on the Judiciary, June 27, 2007. www.heritage.org/Research/Crime/tst082807a.cfm.

National Coalition to Abolish the Death Penalty. "Innocent and Executed: Four Chapters in the Life and Death of America's Death Penalty." https://secure.democracyinaction.org/dia/organizations ORG/ncadp/images/InnocentAndExecuted.pdf.

New York Times. "Cruel and Far Too Usual Punishment," January 7, 2008. www.nytimes.com/2008/01/07/opinion/07mon2.html.

Romero, Gloria. "Death-Penalty System Loaded with Racial Bias," *Los Angeles Daily News*, February 27, 2008.

Russo, John F. "Don't Abandon the Death Penalty, Fix It," *Baltimore Sun*, March 1, 2007.

Segura, Liliana. "200 Executions and Counting: Texas Gov. Rick Perry's Cruel Death Tally," AlterNet, June 2, 2009. www.alternet

.org/rights/140398/200_executions_and_counting:_texas_gov._rick_perry's_cruel_death_tally/?page=entire.

Thomas, Cal. "A Matter of Life and Death," *Human Events,* April 22, 2008. www.humanevents.com/article.php?id=26147&keywords=death+penalty.

Viguerie, Richard A. "When Governments Kill," *Sojourners,* July 2009. www.sojo.net/index.cfm?action=magazine.article&issue=soj0907&article=when-governments-kill.

Williams, Minerva. "What Humanity in the Death Penalty?" *LA Progressive,* June 14, 2006. www.laprogressive.com/2009/06/14/what-humanity-in-the-death-penalty/.

Web sites

Bureau of Justice Statistics Capital Punishment Page (http://bjs.ojp.usdoj.gov/index.cfm?ty=tp&tid=18). This government Web site offers excellent statistical information about the death penalty in the United States. It contains numerous poll results, statistical analysis, and fact sheets about the death penalty, the executed, and those on death row.

Catholics Against Capital Punishment (www.cacp.org). This site provides links and articles on why the death penalty is inconsistent with the Catholic faith.

Clark County Prosecuting Attorney's Office—The Death Penalty (www.clarkprosecutor.org/html/death/death.htm). This exhaustive pro-death-penalty site provides more than a thousand links to articles that both support and oppose the death penalty. A helpful timeline of capital punishment in the United States is also included.

Homicide Survivors.com (http://homicidesurvivors.com/). This site offers articles and posts on why the death penalty should remain legal, focusing mostly on ways in which the death penalty offers justice to the families of victims.

Murder Victims.com (www.murdervictims.com). This site acts as a memorial to violent-crime victims. It serves as a pro-death-penalty resource for murder victim survivors and offers information on murder statistics and the death penalty.

Pro-Death-Penalty.com (www.prodeathpenalty.com). This site has an extensive collection of articles that favor capital punishment, along with helpful links and charts that analyze executions state-by-state. Its section on state death penalty laws is useful.

Students Against the Death Penalty (www.studentabolition.org). Chapters of students who oppose the death penalty exist all around the country. This site contains information for students who want to start a chapter at their school.

Wesley Lowe's Pro-Death-Penalty Web Page (www.wesleylowe.com/cp.html). This site links to several essays that argue in favor of the death penalty and refute points and claims made by death penalty opponents.

Index

Picture Credits

Maury Aaseng, 18, 24, 29, 40, 49, 55, 62, 67, 87, 95, 102, 106, 122
© Alan Schein Photography/CORBIS, 84
AP Images, 10, 13, 19, 31, 43, 45, 47, 54, 60, 66, 77, 81, 88, 94, 100, 108, 113, 120
© Jim Pickerell/Alamy, 36
Brendan Smialowski/Getty Images for Meet the Press, 26